© William J. Harding
First Published in 2010

The views expressed in this book are the author's and may
not necessarily reflect those of related bodies.

Content

The methods and models outlined in this book are a composite of the techniques used by some of the most eminent and respected investigators. The methodology provides the tools for investigators at all levels to conduct a comprehensive and thorough enquiry.

When one respected investigator was asked whether it was necessary to go to such lengths for every investigation he replied;

"Of course experienced and competent investigators will often use their professional judgement. However, they will always consider that it is better to **assess** *that something is the case than to* **assume** *it to be so.... it is my experience that a shortcut more often turns out to be the longest, most complex and painful route to take."*

About the Author

William J. Harding served thirty years with the police. He headed a number of murder investigations and investigations into countless untimely deaths and critical incidents. He has worked on an evidence project with the London Metropolitan Police and with police forces in Europe and the Far East.

In 1997, he completed a psychology related Master of Science Degree in Change Agent Skills and Strategies at the University of Surrey. For ten years, he has studied the relationship between aspects of psychology and the investigation process. From this research, he has developed and used the techniques and models outlined in this handbook.

For the last five years, he has been training investigators from police forces, local authorities and other organisations. The training has met with very positive feedback with many investigators expressing the view that this allowed them to articulate a consistent way of working.

Introduction

This book is intended to provide theory and methods that relate to the investigation of critical incidents such as untimely deaths, missing persons or complex crimes. It includes an explanation of some of the psychological influences on people who are involved in such cases. The book provides a coherent methodology of investigation that can be applied regardless of context; and a number of simple models that can be used during most incidents whether they are simple or chaotic.

As scientific methods and specialist functions are becoming more tightly refined and less open to challenge, there is a greater focus on the conduct of the senior investigators and their approach to the investigation. The theory and models outlined here will enable investigators to articulate clearly their strategies and the rationale for their actions.

The first section of the book identifies the psychological influences that may hinder the progress of an investigation. It endeavours to do this in a partly experiential manner by providing exercises and case studies that the reader can complete to gain first hand understanding of the issues outlined. The case studies are based on real events but, in the interest of sensitivity, the names and some of the details have been changed.

The second section of the book outlines the main theory of investigation that will enable the investigator to overcome any psychological influences that may detract from an efficient, effective and ethical investigation. This section includes an evidence-gathering model that can be used in conjunction with the main theory to ensure that the psychological influences on others can be tested and checked.

In recent years the term investigation has come to have a far wider meaning than the pure gathering of evidence. It includes the effective management of people affected by the events and by the investigator's actions. The effects will range from the impact on those at the immediate scene of the incident or event, to those indirectly affected by the incident itself and by the conduct of the investigators; at times the investigation will have national and international dimensions.

In a society that is more litigation minded the conduct of an investigation is likely to be questioned vigorously and undergo close scrutiny. Many more investigations are also likely to attract media attention and this can be almost instant with live visual and audio broadcasts to audiences around the world. This intense analysis can only add more pressure to the work of the investigators and require them to develop a new range of skills and strategies to deal with it.

The book is not intended to provide an in depth account of theories of psychology, there are many publications that will deal with these issues in more detail. This book does not include details about the technical aspects of the work of experts or specialists who will assist the senior investigators. It is expected that they will have their own existing procedures, protocols and manuals that deal with their specialist matters and there is little value in trying to provide every investigator with a potted guide to, what can be, quite complex matters. Experience shows that the scientific elements of investigation work are developing all of the time; theories are modified on a regular basis; and new technology streamlines many processes; any layperson or past specialist who is not practised and up to date with these may find that they are more of a hindrance than a benefit to the investigation.

At the time of publication many of the manuals, protocols and doctrine written for police investigators attempt to include elements of the work of experts, this can make them overly complex and difficult to use. It also runs the risk of creating a 'tick-the-box' approach to investigations. The 'tick the box' approach can lead to lines of enquiry being followed because they appear on the list and there is a real possibility that their purpose in relation to the strategy of the investigation will be lost. There is also likelihood that, with so much undirected data, the analysis of it will become unmanageable. It is arguable that the best investigators are the ones who can ask the most searching questions against a well-formulated strategy and not the ones who have a smattering of dated knowledge on the intricacies of the specialist work and blindly follow a list of actions that have been prescribed to them.

There are also indications that following lists for list sake can lead to a defensive attitude and risk-averse approach. This can be time consuming and unnecessarily costly. It is quite possible that conducting actions from a defensive standpoint will actually result in the very things that the investigator was seeking to avoid; much like the sportsman who undertakes a tackle half heartedly to avoid injury and places himself at more risk attracting the very injuries that he was trying to avoid in the first place.

When any investigator arrives at a conclusion, one of the key questions for him or her that has emerged over the last decade or so is whether there is another plausible explanation than the one proffered. The investigator should be in a position to demonstrate that all other plausible explanations have been as far as possible eliminated or disproved. Any coherent investigation model should cater for this requirement. The methodology and models outlined in this book will enable the investigator to answer those questions.

Section One

Psychological Influences

An important aspect of any investigation is the psychological influences on people involved in them. The people who may be influenced will include the witnesses to the events; the investigation team; and even specialists who are called upon to support the investigation. It will become clear that these influences are not a result of mental flaws in any of the people involved but merely a product of how, in normal circumstances, the brain and mind works. These influences can have a profound effect on the conduct of the investigation, how evidence is gathered and how it is interpreted.

The psychological influences on witnesses can result in misleading accounts of events and, at the most extreme, can result in witnesses including facts that they have simply not seen or heard. This does not refer to people who deliberately lie to mislead the investigator, but to genuine individuals who are tricked by their own thought processes and provide accounts that can be startlingly inaccurate. The case study in Section 2 demonstrates how, even on a straightforward event, witnesses can be misled in their recollection of events.

It is expected that specialists who support the investigation will be more scientific and highly accurate in the accounts and assessment that they provide. However, recent experience has shown that this is not always the case. Despite their best intentions, specialists can be subject to the same psychological influences as any one else; the infant death cases involving the testimony from Sir Roy Meadows is a startling example of how mistaken an 'expert' can be.

Perhaps the most important person to consider in this aspect is the investigator. It is his or her role to ensure that the information, evidence and accounts that they receive from whatever source are assessed for accuracy, reliability and that they are given the level of consideration that they deserve. The investigator must be sure that the evidence he or she receives is factual and not a product of interpretation or misinterpretation by the witness. It is important in this respect for the investigator to know the source of the information that they receive and to have a means of checking its veracity; later a model that serves this purpose is explored. If the investigator is not alert to their own psychological influences, they can be lead into making inaccurate assessments, taking inappropriate actions and drawing incomplete or premature conclusions.

A Model of How the Brain and Mind Works

Psychologists from most schools recognise that throughout their lives individuals will formulate and modify **'patterns'** about almost everything in their lives. Different psychologists will refer to these as *frames, frames of reference,* or *schemas.* Whilst the label is different, the principle is the same for all of these. They refer to perceptions that are learned through direct experiences and through various forms of socialisation that an individual will receive as they develop. An individual's **patterns** will determine how they interpret just about everything that they encounter from objects, people, situations etc.

The range and depth of patterns is such that a book like this could not do justice to the whole topic; but to give some flavour, things like stereotyping, religious beliefs and moral values would all be examples of patterns or messages that contribute to pattern forming. It will be highlighted later that patterns have particular characteristics and are often set into context; take for instance the 'stealing is wrong' pattern held by a person who brings stationary home from work for their child to use at school. They might not see this behaviour as fitting into the pattern of 'stealing' and have a different pattern such as 'these are perks' to justify what they are doing.

Initially, in childhood, individuals are socialised by parents or parent figures; this is where they formulate their earliest patterns and many of these will be enduring and continue to influence them into adulthood. Take a simple example of eating an evening meal at home. Some people will eat this from their laps in front of the television others will feel uncomfortable about doing this and insist the meal is taken at the table. The people in the latter category are likely to be able to trace this discomfort back to their childhood and

10

parental instruction. Deviating from this pattern, even in adulthood, may still cause the person some anxiety.

The above may be a simple example but the individual's patterns can be highly complex and be deeply ingrained. The more complex form of patterns includes such things as stereotyping where an individual can form quite intricate beliefs about a person or group of people on very little data such as appearance, voice accent or behaviour. This attitude may have been formed through direct contact with someone from the stereotype group but may equally be a result of the views of others.

As individuals grow, their own experiences will add to, reinforce and modify their patterns. It is not however necessary for individuals to have a direct experience of something to form a pattern about it. They can learn about and formulate patterns about things from others who may or may not have had the experience. In the same way, each individual may influence the patterns of others with whom they interact.

A significant amount of pattern learning in adulthood may take place when an individual first joins an organisation or new group and is socialised by the views of current members. This learning may well be integrated with the person's existing views with interesting results and permutations. In some senses, this organisational socialisation can have quite an impact on a newcomer to the extent that they abandon some of their old perceptions in favour of the new learning. It may be difficult to belong to a group and yet hold distinctly different patterns about relevant matters from other, perhaps more senior and respected, members. It is quite possible that, in any organisation, there is significant amount of effort applied to ensuring that patterns are agreed and shared by its members.

Particularly relevant to the subject of this book is the kind of pattern forming that can occur during socialisation into an organisation such as the police where investigation is one of its key functions. This type of organisation deals with incidents that most people are unlikely to have a direct experience of in the early part of their lives, and therefore have had little opportunity to form patterns about its activities. In these circumstances newcomers may be highly reliant on and heavily influenced by the patterns of more experienced members.

It is quite evident and can be seen from the case studies and examples that will follow that there can be a number of shared patterns that are almost inherited by the people who join these organisations. Some theorists might refer to these as the 'culture' or artefacts of the culture. Having made this point it should be borne in mind that, because individuals are unique, even the shared patterns of an organisation are likely to take on a slightly different meaning for each person. This reflects the person individuality and the learning from past experiences that can become entwined with the new socialisation.

When the brain or mind receives some form of stimulus be it visual, audio, kinaesthetic or via any of the senses, it is likely to make a link with one of the stored patterns and interpret the data against that pattern. This is almost an automatic process; Edward De Bono (1990) refers to the brain in this respect as 'a self-organising system' where this patterning activity is used to interpret every piece of stimulus that the individual encounters throughout their daily lives.

There are times when this connection with patterns happens out of the individuals conscious and other times when they make a conscious connection. The patterning process can itself be complex and dependant of different circumstances, which results in the same data being interpreted in different ways or connected with different patterns. The reader will see a useful example of this in the case study that follows, where students state that they are only interpreting things the way they are because the problem is set in a classroom environment and as one student noted, *"We are more careful because it is in here* [the classroom]. This kind of pattern overlapping process where one pattern overlays another is not unusual and makes the analysis of it even more complex.

Patterns (nature and characteristics)

The patterns we form have some distinct characteristics. Some of these characteristics are particularly relevant in the investigation setting. The following is a list of them and what they might mean in terms of investigations:

- ***They have wide catchment areas*** ~ this means that a variety of stimulus could end up with the same pattern being activated. Two people seeing different elements of the same event may report the entire event in the same way if their patterns are similar; therefore a person only seeing the start of an event and another who has only seen the outcome might still give similar accounts of the entire incident. In a classroom exercise various students are given different small parts of the picture of a van, very much like the pieces of a jigsaw puzzle and yet all of them provide a very similar description of the entire vehicle even though they cannot see it in its entirety. A small part of this they gain from the picture the rest they draw from the patterns that they hold in their minds from their experiences. Depending on the person's experiences the description may be more or less complex; so the ex mechanic may provide a far more detailed description of the van than the person who has little direct experience of vehicles. None the less all of them provide a reasonably similar description of the vehicle. It will be seen in the case study that is to follow that eye witnesses seeing an incident from different view points still manage to give a similar description of the whole incident.

- ***The patterns are complete and idealistic*** ~ this means that a small amount of data can activate the whole pattern. A person seeing one part of an event may describe the whole event as if it had actually occurred; some of this will be what they have witnessed and the rest will be made up of the contents of the pattern. In the classroom the students are shown the video of a young man running away from a shop. From this short clip, some of the students use their stereotype experience to observe that the man is a criminal, probably a drug addict stealing things from the shop to buy drugs. They suggest that he is of low intelligence probably living on a council estate. Because the pattern in the mind is so complete, it is possible that people omit or ignore data that does not fit with the details of their particular pattern. This may not be a conscious effort to dismiss data but the fact that they just do not notice it perhaps because it does not seem relevant to their particular interpretation.

- *They have knife-edge boundaries* ~ this means that we are driven to make a selection or choice and it makes it hard for individuals to suspend judgement on what the data might mean or to consider a wide range of possibilities. If someone is not sure they are quite likely to make a choice with their nearest fit pattern than to suspend judgement. This choice of course may be made out of consciousness. It can be seen from the picture exercise in Fig 4 following, that the student's experience does not help them to identify the last picture and many of them will make a guess at what it is. Students are asked to write *"I Do Not Know"* if they cannot recognise an object yet very few of them write this, most resorting to writing a question mark or leaving the space blank. The reason for this may be that there is a strong pattern in the organisation that suggests saying *"I do not know"* is not a sign of strength or professionalism. Over the years that these exercises have been run there are indications that the reluctance to express a lack of certainty is diminishing and members seem more comfortable in saying *"I do not know"* but for many that reluctance still remains.

- *They are unique to individuals* ~ even though there appear to be many shared patterns, the details are still likely to vary from person to person. The detail in an individual's pattern is likely to come from their personal experiences as occurs in the vehicle jigsaw exercise; because we all have slightly different experiences it is not surprising that the details in shared patterns may differ slightly. Some people may add such detail to the account and this can give a false impression of accuracy. As well as the vehicle example, there is strong evidence that people in the investigation

14

arena with the necessary experience can add considerable detail from their pattering process. This can have a double-edged sword effect; on the one hand providing extra clarity if it is based on fact, but on the other, if it is not factually based, it can become misleading and risk an even stronger reinforcement of the pattern.

- ***They are contextualised*** ~ this means that the same data may link to different patterns in different circumstances. Edward De Bono cites the example of a glass being interpreted in most circumstances as a vessel to drink fluids from and it would be difficult for people to consider it as a missile. However, in a 'bar brawl' situation we might well see the glass as a potential missile. In relation to investigations, it is not unusual for people to interpret seemingly innocent behaviour as suspicious against a context of criminal circumstances. In the Dunblain in 1996, some people gave evidence that some years before the offender, Thomas Hamilton, had made a shooting action towards boys with his fingers, they now considered that this might be some indication of his future murder spree. Following a violent crime, the public are used to seeing the loved one of a victim appealing for help on the television; if the loved one seems to fit the pattern of distraught relatives the public may well interpret them as secondary victims. If, however, the relative appears too calm given the traumatic events, people can start to see them as suspects. This different perception or interpretation arises because of the effects of patterns in the circumstances. The 'context' is often made up from many seemingly small elements coming together to provide the overall setting and these are often more difficult for the investigator to distinguish or articulate.

A useful way to think about patterns is to consider that each **pattern** as a jar of beads, where the beads are the contents that make up the pattern. Some of our patterns will have very limited content. Take, for instance, our pattern of a chair, its content is likely to include *a seat, a back, three or four legs. Those legs will sit firmly on the ground and the chair will support our weight when we sit on it.*

From this pattern we will recognise objects as chairs and sit on them; we normally do not test the chair to determine that it will take our weight we trust it from our pattern. There may however be times when we are caused to challenge our pattern of a chair; take for instance the schoolteacher of Form 3A whose boy pupils set up the broken chair in the class to look like a normal chair and the teacher goes to use it to find that it collapses. Because of this experience, this teacher is likely to test her pattern of 'a chair' in the classroom setting in the future although it is unlikely that her pattern of a chair in any other context would change. She may also pass on that experience to her colleagues who may be caused to challenge their pattern of a chair in the setting of Form 3A

Our pattern of a chair however is under constant modification as new models are introduced; we may add the notion a chair with a central stem and splayed feet in the style of a computer chair as a variant within our existing pattern. Of course, some people will have very wide patterns of chairs if they have had experience of a range of different styles. An individual's experience may also cause them to think differently about the 'chair'. For most people it is an object to sit on, however for the designer may take more notice of its shape and the carpenter may be more interested in the wood or its joints.

The chair pattern is clearly a simple example of the notion of patterns and their contents. We do however have far more complex patterns with many more component parts and variants. These include such concepts as stereotyping, morals and beliefs. They also include the sort of life situation that an investigator may encounter; think for example of the complexity of the pattern that we label *'suicide'* and the number of variables that it may hold.

16

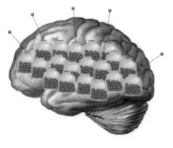

The brain stores thousands and thousands of these patterns during a lifetime and is constantly modifying some with experience. As data is received from the senses the brain attempts to link it to a pre-existing pattern. If it cannot make an exact match it will find the nearest fit. There is likely to be a level of anxiety when a ready fit cannot be found.

The brain will not need the entire image to make a connection; as identified above the wide catchment area enables small amounts of data to enliven the pattern. Using the example of the chair pattern it can be seen that even from this partial image opposite, the brain can make the fit.

The pattern in this case may even include the context that this type of chair will be found in and the whole pattern including context is enlivened. It is often the case that students who see an image or hear a sound bring to mind circumstances from their past that include this data. When listening to a short audio clip of bird songs, one student was able to bring to mind the image of the tree outside her bedroom. She said how annoying the birds could be and how the sound that was being played raised that feeling of annoyance.

Of course, there will be occasions where the brain just cannot make a match to an existing pattern. On these occasions, there is a need to formulate a new pattern to help make sense of the data and this becomes a learning process. That new pattern will become embedded and carried forward to future experiences. The person may also choose to share their new pattern with associates. In the early years of life as children when we encounter new situations, this learning will take place more often.

The frequency of new patterns is likely to increase when the individual encounters situations where they have no comprehension or experience. This is often the case when new investigators enter the field and have very little understanding of the situations that they meet. In these circumstances the investigators ability to interpret data is even more challenged. There is no doubt that their brains will be working overtime trying to make the nearest fit with existing patterns and where they cannot they will be attempting to collect the factors that will lead to the new pattern; and as has been said before they are likely to rely on existing members to help with that process.

The following are some simple exercises that may reinforce the concept of 'patterns' and their characteristics. The exercises have been shown to student detectives and incident commanders, some of their observations are provided in italics.

In Fig 1 below what shapes can you see and how many of each are there?

Fig 1

People have been able to see up to eight triangles, three circles a star; and some younger people may see three 'pac men'. Even though they are viewing the same drawing different people have given different answers and at times there have been significant differences in the answers.

The reasons for some of the findings are to do with the pattern linking process. People who do not have a pattern of 'pac men' tend to see a large white triangle superimposed onto three dark circles hiding a small sector of each. Those people have effectively drawn imaginary lines around their hidden sector to form a complete circle. *Others have seen a white triangle overlaying a large grey triangle. Others will see four small white triangles the tips if which are overlaying black circles.* Figure 2 identifies the invented lines.

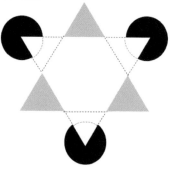

Fig. 2

The reality is that the drawing is only two dimensional but the shapes have been seen in the context of each other and the brain has made a fit with a three dimensional figure; if the context is changed then the interpretation of the shapes changes. In actual fact the picture only contains three grey triangles and three partial circles ('pac men' shapes). The rest has been invented by the individual. Fig 3 below shows the new context exposing the shapes that are actually present.

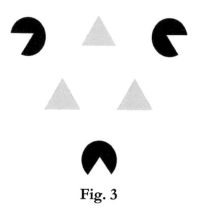

Fig. 3

19

So strong is the desire in some people to make a connection with an existing pattern that even this change of context has encouraged them to try and draw a new set of lines to make a hexagon out of the white area between the grey triangles.

This pattern-making phenomenon can be seen in studying other objects. The below pictures in Figure 4 are useful examples.

Fig. 4

Generally the left picture has been reported by most as a dice and yet in reality there is only a small corner of what might be a dice on view. The remainder of the dice image has been filled in from the pattern of the dice that is held by many people. *The middle picture has variously be described as a camera lens or binoculars* yet again only part of the object is on view. The rest is made up; *some people are even prepared to suggest what make of lens or camera this belongs to.*

The right hand picture might only be recognisable to electrical technicians with some seniority; yet, *generally, people will make some choice about what it is. It has been variously described as a view from an aircraft, a jar of screws or a bottle of something* in reality they guess. This picture has caused some anxiety to those who cannot make a convincing fit with any of their patterns. *Experience, with the trainees has shown that very few are prepared to write or say 'I do not know' when they view this picture.* The reason for this may be to do with the pattern in police service that leads many to believe that saying 'I don't know' is not acceptable; this is the nature of patterns that overlay other patterns.

It is fair to say that not every person on every occasion is making up every detail from every account about an event. It is however reasonable to expect the investigator to test the veracity of the details provided to ensure that the information, account or assessment that he or she has been given is 'fact' and not the result of the minds process and psychological influences. They need to know for sure what are facts and what are filled in details from patterns; they need to know what is 'known' and what is 'a guess'. Investigators need also to be aware of whether they themselves are accessing patterns when; assessing information; giving instructions; and drawing conclusions from events.

Perhaps the most dangerous thing about patterns, particularly in relation to investigations, is that they can become self fulfilling. Data that confirms the pattern is sought and noted; data that tends not to support the patterns can be omitted or disregarded all too easily.

Another great difficulty with the whole process of forming and using patterns is that on many occasions the 'pattern' turns out to be exactly what the individual assumed it to be in the first place. In the pictures on page 20 Fig. 4, it is highly likely that the partial 'dice' or 'camera lens' will turn out to be exactly that. People may then wonder what all the fuss was about in doubting their original assessment, which may in turn lead to a reinforcement of the pattern.

Dangerously however for the investigator there will be times when that pattern assessment turns out to be incorrect which leads to all kinds of problems. Worryingly also is the fact that on some occasions it will never be known whether the assessment based on patterns was correct or not and fundamental errors may go unchecked.

The patterning process can have insidious effects for the investigator in other ways. Perhaps the most difficult to unravel is the notion of what used to be called 'Chinese whispers' where data is modified as it is articulated from person to person. Take for example the picture of the partial dice; students know that they have seen what they believe to be a white plastic or ivory dice. When asked what they had seen, they are likely to make that whole and say 'a dice'.

21

The person receiving this information is likely search their stored patterns and may well make a connection with their red wooden monopoly dice. They tell the next person that the first person saw a monopoly dice, which causes the third to make a connection with their monopoly dice, which may be made of metal or if they do not have one to make the nearest fit. Before long, the original image is now so distorted that it becomes highly problematical for the investigator to unravel the truth, in this case the content of the original picture.

Old Man Case Study

The examples so far have been slightly removed from the context of an investigation but the following case study is an actual incident and will put all of the above concepts into that context. Whilst the incident actually occurred, the names and details have been changed in the interest of sensitivity.

The case study has been shown to many trainee investigators who are asked their views or assessments as the details unfold. The case is presented here in the incremental way that the trainees received it. The reader may find it interesting to plot their own thoughts throughout the study and compare them to the annotated examples from the trainees.

The incident occurred at approximately 9.45 am in a town centre setting, with a two way High Street and a side junction Station Road. On one corner of the junction is Clarks Store and on the other a Café (see Fig 5 page 23). The incident was phoned into the police by a person in Clark's Store and the Police Operator recorded the incident on computer messages as follows: "*Pedestrian –v- lorry. An old man has stepped in front of lorry. Lorry has hit him he seems seriously injured.*" The term 'Pedestrian –v- Lorry…' is recognised short hand for road a collision of this nature.

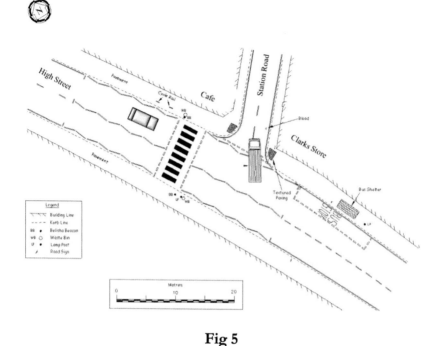

Fig 5

Few members of the public will use these sorts of terms when reporting an incident, however within the police force they are widely used on recorded messages and in radio messages to responding police personnel. Whilst the reasoning for this is 'brevity', the actual affect is to create and cause a responder to access a 'pattern'. It is quite possible that even at this very early stage the quality of the investigation is on an unstable footing.

Having viewed the map and received this early information at least half of the students are prepared to assess that the old man has stepped of the kerb outside Clark's shop and been struck by the lorry. Some are reluctant to commit to any conclusion and readily admit that they feel that there may be some trick or twist to the scenario. They are of course linking the classroom event to another 'pattern' where facilitators seek to draw students into wrong answers.

23

Many of these state that they have not personally experienced such sessions but have heard that they occur.

Some are prepared to say that they are keeping an 'open mind'. When challenged on this some fall back to the non-committal group who suspect a twist. Others stay with the 'open mind' position but are generally unable to articulate what this means. Later when they are asked to articulate their intended actions they become less certain about the 'open mind' position.

There are four independent witnesses to the event as well as the lorry driver. The witnesses are in the car that is shown to the left of the pedestrian crossing. The mother is driving the car, her son is front seat passenger and the son's two friends are rear seat passengers. Students are asked to assess the collision from the information provided (some of their comments are included in italics).

The first account comes from the lorry driver:

Patrick Michael BARKER , 38 years ~ Lorry driver

"I was driving a lorry. I have driven it for a year and a half. Nothing was obscuring my vision. I drove round the one-way system entering the High Street going up it. I then got to Station Road junction where I had to slow right down. I was turning right as I looked down there was a lorry parked on the left hand side of the road which was the wrong side of the road. It forced me over the opposite side. So I actually entered the junction on the wrong side of the road…. I just heard a bang and jumped out of the lorry. I had obviously had a collision with an old man. I didn't see him at all."

This information does not seem to change the position of the students although some question the presence of the other lorry and feel that it may be an excuse for not seeing the old man but generally, they do not see the lorry driver as being at fault.

The next account is from the lady driving the car:

Lorraine Jean JONES ~ Driver of car ~ mother

"I was driving my car. We were in the vicinity of the pedestrian crossing prior to Station Road. When I remember seeing a lorry turn slowly across our lane into Station Road from the High Street and seeing an old man, definitely on the footpath on the Clark's Store side of Station Road. I remember seeing the old man move forward with a jolt and then fall backwards into the road. I did not see the lorry hit the man but it stopped abruptly."

This account seems to confirm the assessment of those who first thought the old man stepped from the kerb at Clark's into the path of the lorry. Some, however, take notice of the word **jolt** *in the penultimate sentence. They start to question whether something has made him move in this fashion and speculate that he may have stumbled or that someone may have pushed him.*

This notion is explored with them and some are prepared to state that in the absence of Mrs Jones mentioning him being pushed they are prepared to dismiss that possibility. However, others remain suspicious and when asked to elaborate on their suspicions some go on to describe the possibility that someone may have tried to steal his shopping bag and in the process, pushed him from the kerb outside Clarks.

Quite clearly, the word **jolt** has activated another pattern in the minds of some of the students and for some the content of the pattern is quite a complex including bag thieves, robbery etc. Interestingly of those who consider the idea that he may have been pushed none of them are prepared to move this incident to an attempted murder investigation.

There are now also one or two trainees who are prepared to question whether the lorry has in fact hit the old man and feel that he may have stumbled and fallen in front of it. This is partly due to wording of the statement and partly a continuing belief that there may be some kind of twist in the scenario.

The next account comes from Mrs. Jones' son:

Jason Peter JONES 14 years ~ front seat passenger

"I was sitting in the front seat of my mother's car. We were in the vicinity of the pedestrian crossing prior to Station Road. I saw ahead of us a lorry turning right slowly across our lane. As the lorry was turning I definitely saw an old man on the footpath on the Clark's Store side of Station Road. He was walking slowly and was walking at a slight angle to the road, but he was definitely walking towards us. I saw him lunge forward and then he was nudged up Station Road by the lorry."

Some people are now concerned about the word **lunge** *and introduce the possibility that he has stumbled on the pavement. They even consider that the pavement may have been uneven and describe how paving slabs can rise or drop and create trip hazards. Some now consider the question of maintenance of the footpath and whether other incidents may have occurred.* These lines of thought have seemingly come from one small piece of data the word **lunge** in the statement of a 14-year-old boy.

The word lunge, for some, evokes the notion that the old man may have deliberately jumped into the path of the lorry. Those who first thought he had stepped in front of the lorry from the kerb outside Clark's store see this account as a reinforcement of that assessment. Some are even critical of those who want to inflate the nature of this incident.

Some of those who were less confident about the potential that he was pushed arising out of the earlier word **jolt,** *now felt that the word* **lunge** *offered a plausible explanation for that type of movement and more firmly ruled out the third party intervention.*

At this point there is normally little evidence of 'sitting on the fence' from those who first thought the exercise might be a trick or hold a twist and in every class everyone contributed actively with some kind of position.

Of those who advocated that they were keeping an 'open mind' many were prepared to maintain that stance. When asked about; the potential of the poorly maintained footpath; the third party intervention; or the step off by the old man; they relied on the 'open mind' fallback. When asked whether they would initiate specific enquiries about the maintenance of the footpath for example, most said they would do so. When asked whether their mind was now focused on that as one possibility and whether they had moved away from the purely 'open mind' position; most felt that they had not.

The next witness was Jason's friend who was the rear off seat passenger who was looking through the front seats:

Charles Michael JACKSON 14 years ~ rear offside passenger

"I was passenger in a car driven by Mrs Jones. I was sitting in the middle of the rear seat. We went over a pedestrian crossing and Mrs Jones stopped to let a lorry turn right across the front of us. I saw an elderly man walking along the footpath. He was travelling in the same way as us. He was just stepping off the kerb outside the Café to cross over to Clark's Store. The man was about two to three steps away from the kerb outside Clark's Store when the lorry hit him."

There is no doubt that this account caused a great deal of confusion for the students. *Those who first thought the old man had stepped out were prepared to say that the witness was quite unreliable for two reasons firstly his age and secondly his restricted vision.*

This statement did however have the effect of resurrecting the 'pattern' of a twist or trick in the exercise for those who were cautious at the start. *Some felt that this might be the very twist that they were expecting and gave considerable weight to the account. Some however gave it less credibility and felt that it was another red herring, to the extent that some have asked if this is actually a statement or something that has been added for effect.* In this, they are further revealing quite a complex pattern of 'classroom sabotage' although very few had ever had direct experience of it happening.

27

The account was 'manna from heaven' for those who were advocating an 'open mind' and for many of these the statement had the effect of withdrawing them from proactive action to test some of the possibilities that they had spoken about earlier.

The last witness in the car was in the rear nearside seat:

Francis Daniel MORRIS 14 years ~ rear nearside passenger

"We were going to Cinema and were being taken by Jason's mum Lorraine. We drove into town and I remember having to stop at a zebra crossing close to the Cafe. I had a fairly clear view out of the front of the car and to the left. I looked ahead and became aware of an elderly man on the pavement he appeared somewhat confused. He was on the far side of Station Road from my position. He walked a few paces up Station Road away from the town and then seemed to turn round a return to the pavement. He then seemed to stumble on the edge of the kerb as if he had just fallen off and he took several short steps. The front of the lorry appeared to hit him and I was shocked to see the man thrown back."

This statement effectively reinforces the accounts of the three other witnesses and exposes the previous witness. *Those who assessed this as a collision where the old man had stepped out from Clark's store feel that this account reinforces that assessment. They point to the detail in the account and felt that this level of detail reflects a far more accurate account. None of these can say that they know of any research that supports this theory and generally, none can remember where or how they have gained that understanding.* This is however another 'pattern' which is affecting their assessment of the reliability of the evidence.

The final account comes from the pathologist:

Dr Johnathan VIGAR BSc, MB.BS., FRC Path. ~ Pathologist

Irregular lacerated wound was present poster laterally on the scalp on the left hand side. Bruising on the scalp particularly posterially on the left and less marked on the right posterially. The skull was fractured. Fracture lines were present in the posterior cranial fossa through the occipital just to the left of the mid line.... In my opinion death resulted from trauma (cerebral lacerations and subdural haemorrhage and a fractured skull). The appearances would be consistent with the history of a road traffic accident.

Trainees who have made different assessments read this report differently. Generally, at this stage of the case study there are three different groups:

The first is the group, who from the outset assessed that the old man had stepped off the kerb from outside Clark's Store into the path of the lorry. *Although the lorry was on the wrong side of the road they believe that there was little the lorry driver could do to avoid the collision and they apportion no blame to him. It is their conclusion that the old man was crossing from Clark's and did not see the lorry, maybe not expecting a vehicle to be on that side of the road. This group are prepared to dismiss the account given by Charles JACKSON because he is young and has a restricted view of the event. This was also the stance they took when his account first appeared.*

This group views the statement of the pathologist as confirming their assessment particularly his conclusion that "The appearances would be consistent with the history of a road traffic accident." *Whilst the majority ask about the damage to the lorry, they are easily satisfied when they are told there was no damage to the lorry. They view the lack of damage and the relatively contained injury sites as an indication that the lorry was not travelling at excessive speed.*

The second group are those who expected the exercise to have some form of twist or a trick. *This scepticism encourages some tentatively to support Charles JACKSON the one aberrant witness because this seems to be the least likely outcome. They find it difficult to dismiss the other witnesses but it is apparent now that they a more intent on avoiding the trap that they imagine exists rather than make a truly held assessment of the incident.*

Most of the final group were those who stated that they were keeping an open mind and they stayed with that position. This group was however very much in a minority, in groups of ten to twelve trainees at a time this has never been more than three people. *When asked to give some form of conclusion they were reluctant to do so, stating that they felt they would need to make more enquiries. They seemed to gain a great amount of justification for this position from the statement of Charles JACKSON.*

When asked what other enquiries they would make, they said that they would seek more witnesses and question the pathologist more about what his findings meant in terms of the behaviour of the old man. When presented with the possibility that another five witnesses might give an account that tended to discredit JACKSON they reserved a right to make an assessment if that occurred. None of this group has felt that a crime had occurred and the investigation should move to 'murder investigation' status. They did not however feel that this compromised their 'open mind' position

No one to date, regardless of his or her position in terms of assessment, has believed that a crime has occurred and the investigation should move to 'murder investigation' status, not even the 'open mind' group. It could be expected that if they were truly open minded they would not dismiss this option. All of those who questioned the maintenance and safety of the footpath failed to raise this in their conclusions. In general, people stayed with or near to their first assessment of the situation. There were, at times, situations where people did not want to move from their first elected position.

What can be seen from the accounts of the exercise is that a vast array of patterns influences the approach of the students. In some cases, it was the 'pattern' of the incident itself. Many of the students will have experienced investigating such a collision or they will have been exposed to the accounts of their colleagues. Call handlers who are unlikely to have experienced such an incident virtually inherit the organisation pattern reflected in the recording 'pedestrian –v- car.' Moreover, there are many such patterns of this type which trigger corresponding behaviours; 'serious RTC *[Road Traffic Collision]* which seems to legitimise high speed travel to the incident; 'cot death' which triggers a sympathetic response to 'Sudden Infant Death Syndrome' and mutes a more disciplined investigation. The list is endless.

Some patterns related to the conduct of the exercise and some students quickly formed the opinion that there was some trick up the facilitator's sleeve; that somehow they were being drawn into making observations that would prove to be foolish. This pattern came close to causing inertia for some in an effort to preserve some form of personal credibility. It is difficult to know the origins of the pattern as most students had not personally experienced such sessions and could not be definite about where they had heard about them.

Then there was the group who advocated 'an open mind'. It is difficult to understand how this can occur and it could be argued that it is another pattern in response to approach to which is encouraged at a national level by such publications as the 'Core Investigation Doctrine'. In effect, it usually seems to limit focussed action and to encourage the search for more and more information, which in itself is not a bad thing but without some focus becomes self-defeating.

The above description tends to portray nice neat defined categories of thought that resulted from the case study. In fact, within the broad categories there were highly individual variations. There is little doubt that in some way each person does influence the others and quite likely modifies other patterns. Some gain from practical considerations concerning the actual case and some have openly reflected that they had never thought about the possibility of this being a trick but they would bring that into the equation on other occasions. Such is the nature of patterns and how they can become shared within an organisation.

The purpose of the exercise, for the Trainee Detectives, is not to see who can solve the case but to allow them to experience how some of their assessments can be the result of other influences than the facts themselves. The reactions highlighted above are typical and there is no reason to believe that they will not continue to be typical with new students. It is after all how the brain and mind works.

It may be easy to believe that such phenomena and reactions can exist in the false setting of a classroom environment and that in reality they are less likely to. Experience however shows that the approaches by the students are replicated in real situations and indeed were so in the actual case that was outlined. Another startling example of this occurred when a call came into a highly specialist police unit about an incident at a particular location; almost in harmony the five officers present predicted exactly what had occurred and how it had happened. Their justification was that some of them had been to *'many incidents'* [8] at this location that it is accepted that the circumstances are likely to be as predicted. In effect when investigators now attend incidents at this location they are highly likely to have made up their minds what the causes were and possibly less likely to challenge those patterns or conduct an objective analysis of the events.

There is no doubt that some of the patterns might be correct from the outset; the picture of the dice and the camera lens in Fig 4 on page 20 will turn out to be just as perceived. On the majority of occasions something an individual assesses as a 'chair' will bear their weight; the dog perceived to be aggressive will attack; and in relation to police incidents on many occasions, they **may** turn out to be as initially assessed.

The word **may** is highlighted above because it is quite clear that pattern linking can have a kind of self-fulfilling prophecy about it. It is evident that once connected it is very difficult to dislodge someone from a particular pattern. It is also clear that they can quite easily dismiss or ignore data that does not support their chosen[1] pattern and gain considerable strength from facts that support their position. It may be the case that many patterns are falsely confirmed through this selective process and therefore become more ingrained. There may also be a strong tendency for an individual to try to prove their chosen position. On other occasions, the patterns go unchallenged and in blissful ignorance, the investigator believes that they had made the correct initial assessment; and so the pattern becomes stronger.

---

[1] The word 'chosen' here should be read with caution this may be on occasions an unconscious process and not a calculated selection by the individual.

The details concerning the actual behaviours of the old man in this incident were not given immediately to the students and all of them expressed some anxiety about moving on until they knew 'the right answer'. It would be interesting to delay this for the reader to test whether the same level of anxiety might occur; however, there may be more value in exploring the position of the various witnesses against the patterning theory. It should be reinforced that any observations here are made tentatively because there was not opportunity to further question in depth the people involved.

The actual investigators in the case explored the area for Closed Circuit Television evidence and found an active camera in the café. The camera overlooked the entire junction and captured the scene of the collision. It revealed the old man walking slowly but quite steadily along the footpath past the café towards the road. The old man stepped quite steadily off the footpath outside the café and crossed the road toward Clark's store. He was carrying a bag of shopping and walking quite steadily although still at the slow pace. He was a few paces from the kerb outside Clark's when the lorry which was moving at slow speed struck him on his right side and knocked him a short distance along Station Road. It is apparent that he struck the left side of his head on the road surface.

In this case, the only reliable witness to the events was Charles Jackson who was completely at odds with the accounts of the other people in the car. The most provocative questions are how the other witnesses can have got things so wrong. None of the people in the car knew the lorry driver or the old man and therefore had no obvious reason to mislead deliberately the police about the events. It therefore has to be the case that other things have caused them to recall wrongly, what occurred. It must be emphasised that no solid conclusions can be drawn from this but it is quite possible that they were reporting on partly what they saw and partly on patterns that they had accessed at the time or later. It may be possible to speculate what these might be.

It is evident that Mrs. Jones had not seen an actual event like this before, however like all motorists she probably has taken notice, over the years, of the many television road safety campaigns that show people stepping out into the path of cars from their nearside leaving the unsuspecting motorist little chance to avoid the collision. Some campaigns implicitly accept the inevitability of the collision and urge drivers to slow down to minimise the amount of injury sustained by the pedestrian. To date none of the campaigns has shown the pedestrian cross from the offside of the road and almost complete their crossing before being struck. It is not difficult to see how a pattern can be established even though one has not had a direct experience of an event. Mrs Jones will have seen the final position of the old man near to the kerb outside Clark's and it is not difficult to understand how that small piece of data could have triggered the pattern and perception that the old man crossed near the lorry.

It may not be as likely that Jason Jones took a similar level of notice of such television campaigns and may not have such an imbedded pattern of pedestrian related collisions. It transpired, however, that Jason was present when Mrs. Jones gave police her account. It is also a requirement for an appropriate adult [normally a parent] to be present when juveniles give a statement to the police. In this case Mrs. Jones acted as that appropriate adult and was present throughout Jason's statement. This raises a range of possibilities about patterns that may have impacted on Jason; these might include 'mum is the driver she knows best'; or 'it is not right to disagree with parents' etc. Some of this may be reinforced by the fact that the two statements are remarkably similar in wording; whether this was mother's influence or the influence of the officer who took both statements it is difficult to know.

Francis' statement is far more complex in relation to the behaviour of the old man, who he says "...*walked a few paces up Station Road away from the town and then seemed to turn round a return to the pavement. He then seemed to stumble on the edge of the kerb as if he had just fallen off and he took several short steps...*" It is difficult to know how he has arrived at this description, but it is clear that he had chance to talk to Jason between the event and the week before he made his statement. There may well be a number of patterns in operation that gave rise to the account; if this is not the case it is difficult to understand how he could have arrived at an account so far from what actually happened.

Perhaps the one person who the investigators rely on to provide information that is based purely on fact is that of Dr Jonathan VIGAR BSc, MB.BS, FRC Path. His title alone with all of the letters related to qualifications is likely to create a perception (pattern) of scientific competence. In fact, much of this report is factually based although the fact that it is couched in medical terms alone is likely to hamper assessment by the investigator and deter any kind of challenge.

The real difficulty comes with his final comments *"In my opinion death resulted from trauma. The appearances would be consistent with the history of a road traffic accident"*. This tends to suggest that it fits with his pattern of 'a road traffic collision', but it practical terms he has allowed and possibly encouraged any investigator to make a connection with their personal patterns of such 'a road traffic collision'. In the same way the passed on description of the dice earlier could evoke a range of interpretations the notion of 'a road traffic accident' may be different for the different people involved and it is not difficult to understand how things can become misinterpreted.

It is clear from the CCTV evidence that the account of Charles JACKSON is very close to reality despite him having a limited view from his position in the car. The key question is how he has stayed free from the pattern linking process that his friends and the mother have experienced. It is interesting to note that shortly after the collision he went away on holiday and was not in contact with Jason JONES or Francis MORRIS. Jackson's statement was taken some weeks after the others and time does not seem to have diminished his recollection of events. Perhaps the absence of any other person's patterns and the lack of any pattern of his own have caused him to absorb the incidents as they occurred and created a learning experience. It would be interesting to know whether this experience has created a new pattern in his mind and how this might affect his account if he were unfortunate enough to see another similar event.

The old man case study and reactions of the investigators is not untypical and not limited to police investigations. A similar example was seen in a Health and Safety Investigation where the opening comments by an engineer to the investigator were, '*This is typical of the internal switch failure causing the motor to run on.*' In actual fact there was a more serious lack of maintenance which caused the machinery malfunction. Similarly an accountant's prior assessment of a financial discrepancy being '*..a failure to carry sub balances forwards, a typical book keeping error*', turned out to be systematic embezzlement over a number of years. The reason for the two experts' miscalculation was based purely on experience that had formed, for them, a 'pattern'.

The patterning system is not restricted to lay people with little training in investigation. Recent history has shown how trained investigators are apt to draw premature conclusions by assuming that the circumstances they encounter are similar to previous events. Some of these cases have attracted strong scrutiny not always because they arrived at an incorrect conclusion but because they were unable to rule out other possibilities.

The patterning process of the mind can also have an impact on specialists such as scientists. Consider the case of a thirty-year-old man who was riding his motorcycle along a semi rural road. A car emerged from a driveway and the motorcycle rider struck its front wing sending him over the bonnet. His head hit the road on the other side of the car and he died. Collision investigators used damage evidence and the account of the other driver to estimate his speed as moderate. They were puzzled by the fact that he appeared to have had time to take avoiding action but had not done so.

The investigator's minds were put at rest when his blood toxicology results came back from the laboratory. The scientist had found traces of the chemicals that were the constituent parts of the controlled drug heroin. The scientist's report included the fact that '*the amount was sufficient to render a lethal dose and that it indicated that the sample was consistent with a drug user*. There were however two difficulties with this report. Firstly, that despite having a lethal dose of heroin in his body the man was still riding a motorcycle. Secondly, there was nothing in his life style that indicated he was 'a heroin user'. Unfortunately, his body had been cremated and direct examination was not possible.

A second scientist from an independent laboratory confirmed the findings and gave an explanation for the high dose reading. A check with the second scientist revealed that when heroin is used by the body it produces a metabolite; however this level of testing is not carried out because the initial findings have **in the past** proved sufficient to indicate heroin **use**. In the parlance of this section in the minds and assessment of the scientists, the '*drug user*' pattern had been established by the first set of tests. When the advanced test was carried out on the sample from the young man, it was found that the metabolite was not present.

There are a number of possible explanations for this, which are listed as follows:

1. The drug was given to the motorcyclist during his treatment at the roadside or at the hospital. Enquiries revealed that he was not given any medication during this period. This option can be disproved.

2. There had been a mix up with the samples and the sample reported was not the motorcyclist's blood. Through DNA analysis with other sources of blood known to be his, the blood sample was confirmed to be the motorcyclist's blood. This option could be disproved.

3. The machine used in the analysis was misread, in some way faulty or contaminated. The readings were checked and had been read correctly. The machine was tested; it was purged, calibrated and found to working correctly. This option could be disproved.

4. The blood had become contaminated between it being taken at the mortuary and analysed at the laboratory. The seal at the sample was recorded as 'in tact' when it arrived at the laboratory. There was nothing found at the laboratory that could have contaminated the blood. This, however, was not the case at the mortuary where the personnel and the technique for taking the blood could have caused the contamination. This could not be proved but with all other options disproved, it was safe to conclude that this was how the heroin came to be in the blood.

The presence of the blood was clearly not through **drug use** by the motorcyclist. The scientists had applied the *pattern* when reporting the findings of the blood analysis based on years of analysing blood samples and finding those chemicals.

The difficulty was not in the findings of the scientists but in the way the report was worded. The report stated that the findings were consistent with '*a drug user*' implying the use of drugs when in fact that level of test could only support the finding of the '*presence of heroin*'. It was only the metabolite test that would justify the term '*use of heroin*'.

Both scientists acknowledged that there was a time that the second level of testing was carried out and the metabolite had always been present and now, only in challenged cases would they look for it. Despite the absence of the second test all reports continued to include the conclusion about drug usage. It was clear that the scientist would understand the limitation of the report but there is little doubt that it stimulated other patterns in the minds of the collision investigators and allowed them to draw inaccurate conclusion about the motorcyclist's case.

This section has considered the notion of 'patterns' as a way of interpreting data. The examples given have involved pattern use in what can be described as a 'direct' way; where people have witnessed an incident or part of incident or event and interpreted it against their past experiences or where analysis has yielded results that have again be compared and interpreted against previous experiences. However, it is also clear that the patterning process can occur in an 'indirect' way and have a significant impact on the quality of investigations.

Indirect patterning may be associated more with the setting or context of the investigation or with the 'cultural' issues that surround it. Take for example the culture of an organisation where senior people criticise operators who, in their assessment, over elaborate or inflate investigations and it may be found that a 'pattern' of playing down enquiries may be applied to avoid criticism. This approach might also be evident when seniors praise those who 'keep things simple' and 'get quick results'. In the same sense when seniors disproportionately criticise operators for minor mistakes, may result in risk-averse investigators who apply a 'tick the box' approach to avoid criticism. Some academics might class these as the 'artefacts of a culture'.

Consider also the broader cultural issues where a particular group of people behave in a way that is considered appropriate in their culture but has a different meaning in another setting. Take for instance a group of people who consider direct eye contact with the person they are speaking with to be disrespectful and another group who believe lack of eye contact to be a sign of dishonesty or suspicious. Similarly, consider a group of people who believe it to be rude to contradict elders compared to another group who consider a lack of input as an acquiescence or tacit agreement. When these conflicting behavioural patterns are present as part of an investigative process the interpretation can have significant impact on its effectiveness.

The nature of patterning whether the 'direct' or 'indirect' type, includes the facts that it is multi facetted operating at so many different layers. It is also evident that it can be applied in a way that is not conscious to the individual. These elements make it hard to detect whether something is known fact or whether it is a result of some person's patterns. There is little doubt that this is one of the priority processes in any professional investigation regardless of context.

Perhaps the most difficult elements of the process is that quite often the pattern turns out to represent closely reality; or on occasions people get that perception because they put little effort into testing or disproving the patterns which results in them being reinforced for the next occasion. This means that on a large number of occasions 'patterns' go unchallenged. The more this happens the more likely it is that the pattern gains strength. There may be times, as with the blood testing, that the pattern has become so strong that any means of testing it have been dispensed with. When the 'pattern' is couched in terms of a 'theory' or 'scientific deduction' the issue for the investigator without specialist knowledge becomes more difficult.

Day to day this patterning process is a necessity. It would be totally impractical and unmanageable for a person to challenge or test every piece of stimulus that they came across. However, it can be seen that the way the brain and mind works can be detrimental to the conduct of an efficient, effective and professional investigation. At the more serious level of incident the quality of data analysis and the need to constantly challenge patterns becomes imperative. The efficiency of the investigation and its subsequent outcome can have such powerful impact on so many people. It is therefore essential that investigators learn how to modify their own thought processes and minimise the adverse affects of the pattern linking by others be they witnesses, specialists or co investigators. Section Two proposes a model that will enable this.

Section Two

Investigative Strategy

'Section One' has outlined how the brain and mind's natural processes of interpreting data can have a detrimental impact on the conduct of investigations. At the time of printing, the national bodies for police investigations in the United Kingdom had issued a number of documents and manuals that try to overcome this. Their approach in some documents was confusing; varying from an encouragement to keep an 'open mind' in relation to murders; to an encouragement to consider the worst-case scenarios (murder and unlawful killing) in the case of missing persons and road deaths respectively. No doubt the latter was intended to stimulate the most thorough of investigations which would of course refer the investigator back to the murder manual that advocated an 'open mind' but in reality it presents a disjointed view of investigation methods and encourages a kind of rivalry between contexts.

Regrettably, neither a demand to 'keep an open mind' or an urge towards the most serious scenario will contribute to a better level of investigations nor overcome the issues relating to data interpretation that have been outlined. It has already been identified that the brain and mind acts as a self-organising system and selects the best-fit pattern to make sense of data that it receives through any of the senses. On many occasion this process takes place out of consciousness, which contributes to the difficulty for individuals to change this in some way.

Without this sorting process, it would be almost impossible for individuals to live their lives; they would have to assess consciously every bit of sensory stimulus before taking action. Add to this the considerations that on a day-to-day basis individual's assessment of familiar situations are reasonably accurate and the consequences of making mistakes are rarely drastic; there is little incentive for people to challenge their own thought processes. Think also of the emotional strength needed by an individual to resist the kind of cultural pressures identified earlier.

Regardless of the real difficulties of preventing the patterning process, it could also be argued that to do so would carry the risk that the knowledge, skills and attitudes of investigators developed over years of experience could be muted and at worst lost from the investigation. During any investigation, and particularly the more complex types, a vast amount of data is produced. To suspend this data in the mind until all of the evidence is assembled seems to be an unmanageable task and is the psychological equivalent of trying to turn back the tide; as we have seen individuals want and at times need to make some kind of interpretation of the data that they are receiving.

It is also the case that, in most situations, not all data or evidence relevant to the investigation is immediately forthcoming or immediately revealed to the investigator, much it has to be sought proactively. Real life investigations are not like a laboratory setting where all of the data has been laid out for the scientist's analysis and conclusions. It is also unlikely that entirety of the evidence sought can be included in a catch all list that the investigator can work through systematically before arriving at their final hypothesis.

It is arguable that the stimulus to search for the relevant evidence are the very patterns (or hypotheses) that the police investigator is discouraged from using. For example, take the situation where a small baby is found dead in his or her cot, unless at the outset the investigator considers 'neglect' (a hypothesis) to be one of the possible causes of death, there would be little motivation to look for appropriate forms of food and nourishment in the kitchen cupboards.

It might, in this example, be argued that the post mortem might reveal such neglect, but by that time the scene is likely to have been released and potential to look for other evidence might be lost for good or its integrity challenged if it was found later. Similar observations could be applied to other possible causes of the child's death and the corresponding evidence to test whether they are viable or not.

The essentials of any investigation methodology must therefore be fourfold:

- Investigators must be discouraged from arriving at early conclusions drawn from their past patterns.
- Investigators should be encouraged to utilise the knowledge, skills and experience that they have acquired over the years.
- The methodology should enable the investigator to demonstrate that he or she has considered all other plausible explanations and whether they have been disproved.
- The methodology should be applicable in all contexts.

It is desirable that the methodology is transparent allowing open scrutiny both during the process of the investigation and at a later time. It should be straightforward and simple to use particularly given the complex and chaotic circumstances of some investigations. Ideally, it should be applicable to all aspects of the investigation from initial scene management, through evidence gathering, to the proactive testing stages.

A methodology that advocates a tick the box approach and is tailored to specific types of investigation does not meet all of the above criteria. The lists of functions can never cover every eventuality and does little to provide a framework to help the investigator to analyse the data; particularly the vast amount of material that is sought and gathered in a complex enquiry.

Hypotheses Model

The methodology that fits the four essential criteria and the desirable qualities highlighted above is the 'Hypotheses Model'. It is a model that recognises that the lifeblood of proactive investigations are the 'patterns' and their contents that were identified in Section One. The use of 'hypotheses' moves the investigation from the fairly static position advocated by the 'open mind' approach where data is collected en masse and interpretation made when data collection is complete; to a proactive level where specific data is sought to test one or more particular 'patterns' or 'hypotheses'. For convenience and continuity, 'patterns' will be referred to from this point on as 'hypotheses'. This is purely a 'label' change because in all other respects 'patterns' and 'hypotheses' are the same.

The 'Hypotheses Model' has two guiding principles that, if followed, will help the investigator to avoid drawing premature conclusions drawn from patterns; provide a comprehensive investigation that is transparent and open to scrutiny. The first principle of the 'Hypotheses Model' advocates that the investigator, from the outset, list **all** of the potential hypotheses that could apply to the presenting context. It recognises the fact that inexperienced investigators may not be able to identify a full range of potential hypotheses and encourages them to consult with their investigation team and other experts in the field.

The list of hypotheses provides the investigator with a framework against which evidence and data can be sought and once gathered can be analysed. In the very early stages of the investigation, it is possible that the investigators will formulate the hypotheses in their heads but they will be encouraged to record them in writing as soon as practicable thereby making their thought processes open for contribution and scrutiny. An example of the listing process can be seen below in relation to the case study of the old man detailed in Section One.

From the outset, the investigator is encouraged to articulate the hypotheses in the following way:

Working Hypotheses
1. *The old man walked in to the path of the lorry and a collision was unavoidable* **(road accident)**
2. *The manner of the driving by the lorry driver contributed to the collision* **(dangerous driving)**
3. *The old man deliberately placed himself in the path of the lorry intending self*

> *harm or death* **(suicide)**
> 4. *The old man was affected by a condition that caused him to go into the path of the lorry* **(medical)** *or* **(neglect)**
> 5. *A third party caused him to go into the path of the lorry* **(crime)**

It can be seen that this range of possibilities differs considerably from the thought processes of the previously mentioned trainee investigators who variously; concluded that this was a road accident from the beginning; thought that there was some kind of trick to the whole exercise; and advocated that they were keeping an 'open mind'. It could be argued that these hypotheses cover all of the foreseeable circumstances that led to the death of the old man. However, in the eventuality that they do not account for it, other hypotheses can be added as information and data is gathered. Where the investigator is receiving data consistently, that does not appear to relate to any of his listed hypotheses; or where the data disproves all of those that he has listed, he can be sure that there is a hypotheses that he has missed.

A useful example of this adding occurred some years ago in circumstances where a person had died by fire. The most obvious hypotheses were that the deceased took their own life; that someone known to the person killed them; that person unknown to them killed them; or that death was accidental. These four hypotheses should have covered the circumstances; however in some cases evidence and data was emerging that did not apply to these hypotheses. Scientist discovered a phenomenon of '*spontaneous human combustion*' where human beings caught fire in an unexplained way. Whilst not all scientists agree the reasons for this, there is little doubt that today diligent investigators could consider this as a hypothesis when dealing with a death by fire.

With reference to the 'Hypotheses Model', it can be seen that listing the potential hypotheses virtually forces the investigator to challenge the first and closest fit that they may make. They are encouraged to ask themselves '*What else could this be?*' Whilst it is clear that the range of hypotheses available to an individual will be dependent on their own range of experiences, they should consult with others to establish a wider range of options. The consultative process does not abrogate the lead investigator from accepting accountability for the working hypotheses but it does help him/her to conduct a comprehensive and inclusive form of investigation.

The second principle of the 'Hypotheses Model' is that investigators are encouraged to try to disprove the hypotheses by testing the presence or absence of the constituent parts of each one. It is not intended that investigators set out to prove a chosen hypotheses, which leads to inappropriate weighting of information. The disproving activity discourages investigators from trying to confirm their preferred 'pattern' or 'hypotheses' and the written articulation of other possibilities help reviewers and observers to check the integrity of the lead investigator. This written articulation is the main factor in establishing the desired '*transparent investigation*'.

In terms of applying the model, there is a preferred technique. It is important that hypotheses are not developed 'series' (as indicated in Fig 5 below. This means that the investigator should not consider one hypothesis gathering data to test it disprove it and then move on to the next most likely hypothesis and disprove that and so on.

A	B	C	D	E

Fig 5

The hypotheses should be run in 'parallel' as indicated in Fig 6 below. What this means is that all hypotheses should be considered at the outset of the investigation, lines of enquiry focus on testing all of the hypotheses and data is assessed against each one. If four hypotheses are listed each piece of data is received with the question, "What does this tell me about each of my hypotheses?" in particular does it help me to eliminate any of them.

47

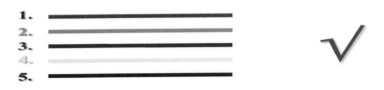

Fig 6

There are significant drawbacks of running hypotheses 'in series', that is starting with hypothesis one; discovering that it can be eliminated and then running on to hypothesis two; and finding the same result before moving on to hypothesis three and so on. The drawbacks of this approach include the fact that time is wasted and that some forms of evidence are either not retrievable after a lapse in time or their integrity is jeopardised by the time gap. Evidence gathered for one hypothesis may also be applicable to the others and with some thought comprehensive tasking can be achieved; whereas tasking to test just one hypothesis can be far less productive and often mean revisiting evidence sources, which can result in complications that could have been avoided.

It can be seen that developing the hypotheses in 'parallel' and completing the next stage of the model will result in focussed activity and economic use of resources. More importantly, running the hypotheses in parallel gives the investigator an opportunity to initiate the priority actions that may save life or property and to preserve the most fragile of evidence.

Take for example the missing child where investigators first consider that the child has run off. Some time could be spent searching. If the child is found, all is well and good; if however they are not found the investigators may start to consider that the child may have been kidnapped and taken out of the area. Early actions would include a systematic check on exit routes; however, the delay through the initial searching makes this a less productive and potentially futile exercise. If, after some days, these enquires bring no result the investigators may consider that the parents, relatives or their associates may have been involved in the child's disappearance. The delay makes any forensic work or story checking highly problematic.

If the hypotheses were run 'in parallel', the investigator would still initiate the search to determine whether the child had run off and the searchers could be tasked to consider also evidence that might test the other hypotheses. At the same time as initiating the search, the investigator could set up checkpoints at appropriate places given the time of the last confirmed sighting of the child. This would undoubtedly enhance the chances of intercepting an abductor. By the same principle, the investigator would immediately preserve the premises where the child was for forensic analysis to test the possibility that something untoward may have occurred there leading to the injury and/or disappearance of the child. They might also conduct a thorough search of the premises in case the child never left.

By applying the 'in parallel' approach the investigators have given themselves a better chance of minimising the impact of the situation and successfully eliminating one or more of the hypotheses. By eliminating such hypotheses as the possibility that the relatives or friends were in some way involved in the child's disappearance, they are likely achieve a number of secondary objectives. They may take a considerable amount of pressure off the relatives who might otherwise be suspected of involvement by uninformed spectators; they could free up resources to concentrate on more viable hypotheses; and they could release specialist services to deal with other, equally demanding, tasks.

As well as the immediate considerations concerning safety, risk and evidence preservation, the 'in parallel' approach maximises the use of resources. In relation to the 'old man' example above, the investigator can task any one of his/her teams to conduct a range of enquiries from the same source that are designed to test the listed hypotheses.

A useful example of this might be enquiries with the old man's General Practitioner or doctor. The team could be asked to gather data that might indicate a motive self harm such as previous attempts, old unexplained injuries; at the same time they could enquire about conditions that might mean the old man is unstable on is feet or prone to collapse unexpectedly; questions could be designed to check for conditions such as poor hearing and poor eyesight that might effect his judgement in crossing the road etc. These examples are not exhaustive but it can be seen that this comprehensive approach can minimise the number of repeat visits to one source which might be the case when the *'in series'* approach is adopted.

Hypotheses Content

Each hypothesis, as listed, is a broad description of what may have occurred in the incident. Each of the hypotheses will have detailed content in much the same way as our broad description of 'chair' outlined earlier. The 'chair' example with its seat, back, legs etc. has fairly simple content; however each detail will still vary according to circumstances; so the 'deck chair' will have different legs to the 'regency dining chair'.

The investigation hypotheses content will also vary in different circumstances; for example in the case of suicide, one of the contents might include a note indicating the person's intentions. In the case of the old man example earlier that note might take the written form whereas a teenager in the same circumstances may have left their note on a computer or social networking site. The compiling the potential content of any hypothesis is an evolving process. The more experienced the investigator becomes, the more beads he or she can add to any of the hypotheses.

In an ever changing world the potential for new and changing elements to occur in such situations is inevitable. The example of intimation of self harm or of intended violent conduct through social media sites is a prime example of how content and subsequent investigation enquiries develop. Experience shows that the content of any of the working hypotheses can change throughout the progress of the investigation. As new information and evidence emerges the

50

investigator may find that new elements are added or that others can be eliminated or discounted.

The content of many investigations are likely to include the actions of individuals, environmental factors, recorded information and specific objects that may be present or absent. It would be impossible for the investigator to list all variations in terms of content and arguably, it would be a mistake to attempt to do so. Many of the details will only be identified in consultation with specialists in the particular context or with other team members who have experience of similar situations. The fluent nature of human situations makes it more important for investigators to evaluate constantly the factors that arise and ask themselves what they say about the viability of any of the working hypotheses.

To give a flavour of what the contents of a hypothesis might look like in practical terms, in the Old Man Case Study 'Hypothesis 3' above could be unpacked as follows:

Content Hypothesis 3~ It was the old man's intention to self-harm or take his own life.

- *He had a motivation to take his own life*
  - *Financial worries*
  - *Terminal or debilitating illness*
  - *Guilt following some act*
  - *Grief or bereavement*
  - *Loneliness*
  - *Failed relationship*
- *He had left a note or some form of message to this effect*
- *He had told or intimated to someone that he was in such a mental state*
- *He had made previous attempts*
- *He cancelled future engagements*
- *He cancelled orders such as milk papers*
- *He recently made or modified a will*

> - *He ensured that his affairs were tidy including paying bills prematurely*
> - *He had attended his GP with related symptoms*
> - *His actions appeared deliberate i.e. looking round and waiting for the lorry*

Fig 7

Each hypothesis represents a 'pattern' that was highlighted earlier. It was identified that a useful way to think of 'patterns' was to picture a pot of beads. In unpacking the hypothesis it can be considered that a single bead represents one element of the contents. Using the above example, the second bullet point '*a note or message*', would be one bead.

All of our hypotheses could be considered in this way and the diagram Fig. 8 on page 53 provides a visual representation of how the investiagtor might see their hypotheses. It will be noted that some coloured beads (or hypotheses content) are common to all of the hypotheses and some are unique. The same can be found in actual investiagtions there will be some data that is equally applicable to more than one hypothesis; for example a set of injuries may equally be applicable to a murder, a suicide and an accident.

The content concerning the listed example in Fig 7 is not exhaustive and it is likely that not all of the elements will be present. The list is a construction of the experiences of the author and it can be made more comprehensive by consulting with team members or specialists in the field. The items in Fig 7 represent some of the content of the 'pattern' labelled '*suicide*' set in the context of this case study. In other circumstances, the pattern will contain other details. If a significant number of the elements expected in a 'hypothesis' are missing (in this example, of self-harm or suicide), the investigator can make the decision to close this as a working hypothesis. Therefore, if there is no note, no previous attempts, no motive etc.; the investigator could conclude that this was not a case of self-harm or suicide.

The same examining process can be applied to all of the hypotheses to determine which can be disproved and therefore closed. This allows resources to be applied to possibilities that are more viable. Each piece of data or evidence is analysed in relation to the working hypotheses to determine its relevance to them and whether they allow some to be closed.

By laying out the hypotheses and the content of each, the investigator is provided with lines of enquiry or actions.

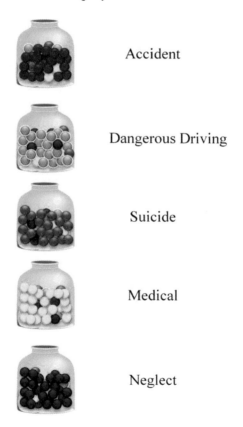

Accident

Dangerous Driving

Suicide

Medical

Neglect

Fig. 8

This step-by-step analysis is not as demanding or as complex as first appears because enquiries and data obtained can be applicable to more than one hypothesis the example of the old man's medical records provide an example of this (see page 51).

Experience tends to indicate that not all of the beads have the same weighting in respect to a particular hypothesis. Some aspects are far more important than others and their presence or absence may have a strong influence in the assessment process. The presence of an item(s) might not prove a particular hypothesis but might disprove others. A useful example of this in relation to suicide would be the presence of a note that expresses the person's intentions where it can be proved that the person wrote it without any third party duress. The presence of the note could not rule out the possibility that the final act was not intended to inflict fatal injuries and that they were not accidental, but it does appear in many instances to rule out murder as a viable hypothesis.

It is not unusual for investigators in particular fields to find that they are formulating similar hypotheses for similar types of incident. By the same token it is not unusual for the content to be similar. In this respect the investigator must be alert to the patterning process that may occur in such circumstances both when listing possible content and assessing evidence against it. It might however be worth noting at this stage that where there is a deliberate act, the investigator can expect to find that the content includes what could be labelled as the 'Three **M**'s'; that is **M**otive, **M**eans and **M**ethod.

For **Motive** the investigator can look initially to the dictionary definition of '*a reason for doing something*'. In relation to investigations the reason normally involves some form of intended outcome by the person initiating the action. Whether at the extreme end this involves suicide or murder or in less extreme circumstances such as burglary or fraud, the investigator can expect that motive forms part of the hypotheses content.

However it is possible that 'motive', in these circumstances, includes not only the intended outcome but the motivation to do so in a particular way; that how the outcome is achieved is appropriate in the circumstances. For example the motive to take ones own life might include things like avoidance of debt, to evade prosecution or punishment, to foreshorten suffering in the cases of terminal illness (again the list is not exhaustive). Beyond that the individual may have particular reasons for choosing the way that they achieve that outcome.

Motive is very much to do with the thought processes of the individual involved and what is in their mind at a particular time. The investigators must be alert to the possibility that they [the investigators] may apply some form of rationality to the notion of motive and accompanying actions. However, by their very nature the acts investigated can often be irrational both in intention and they way they are carried out.

It can be difficult for an integrated functioning person to understand how one human being can be motivated to kill another; or an individual take their own lives; or in the case of a suicide bomber perform both of these acts. It may be even harder to understand that the motive may be, in the investigator's view, as trivial as the fact the one person lives in a different post code to the other.

In cases where delusionary people are involved 'motive' can be even more difficult to understand; take for example the case of Eric Bikubi and Magalie Bamu, who killed 15-year-old Kristy Bamu in their East London flat after violently abusing him for several days because they said they thought he was a sorcerer. If they are to be believed, understanding that kind of motive can become a real challenge for the investigator and compiling the hypothesis content even more challenging.

In the three M's, **Means** relates to the things that are needed to carryout the deliberate act. In cases of violence these might include the weapon and investigators would ask whether the suspects in cases of third party violence or the victim in self administered violence could have access to the type of weapon used. Again it would be too exhaustive to cover the equipment and object issues in more detail and each case will be assessed by the investigator. However, 'Means' includes less tangible things like the time to do the acts or the opportunity to do so. It would also include the information needed. Take an elaborate computer identity or financial fraud; the investigator would consider who had the necessary equipment, pass words, access to the systems and time to complete the transactions. All of these things would be covered under the heading of 'Means' for the hypothesis content.

Method in this context refers to the technique used and skills and ability needed to apply that technique. In the fraud case above, certain computer hacking skills might be needed or an ability to change computer records. In a death by hanging the investigator would ask for instance whether the deceased person could have tied the knot themselves or physically got themselves into the final position. In some instances the number of people related to an investigation who would have the necessary skills and ability might be numerous but the more elaborate and technical the Method the less people would fit that profile. These things would be assessed on a case by case basis and probably with the help of specialists.

The model demonstrates how difficult it can be to have a 'tick box' list of evidence for every sort of case. It shows the value of using the past experiences of the investigation team and any consulted specialists. The essence of the model is that, action and enquiries are set for specific purposes to test the viability of one or more of the hypotheses. If a number of significant elements are missing then the investigator can, with a level of confidence, close the particular hypothesis. It is quite often the case that one or more hypotheses can be eliminated quite quickly particularly when significant parts of the content are missing. There is however nothing to stop the investigator reopening a hypothesis if the evidence countermands the previous decision to close it.

This hypotheses building and filtering process can be carried out at all stages of the investigation. Initially the hypotheses will be broad and about the context of the incident for example murder, suicide, accident etc. If all hypotheses but murder are eliminated, that hypothesis can be refocused on things like a potential list of suspects where the hypotheses related to motive, means or method are further explored. It should be emphasised that this does not normally mean a brand new evidence gathering process and more likely be an evolving process from the evidence that has already been gathered.

In summary, the investigator will have a number of working hypotheses and for each one they will have considered, in some detail, what the content of the hypotheses would include given the context of the investigation field. They will then set actions to test the presence or absence of the content elements of each of the hypotheses with a view to closing them down. Of course, some data will be forthcoming even though actions have not been set. All incoming data should be analysed to determine what it tells the investigator about the viability of any of the working hypotheses. The investigator will also consider whether any of the data is indicating a hypothesis that has not been included in the initial assessment.

The Hypotheses Model should be applied from the very outset of the response to the incident or event. This will enable the person in charge to consider actions designed to minimise danger and risk as well as actions designed to gather evidence about the circumstances of the matter under investigation. The Hypotheses provide a framework to direct the gathering and the analysis of data. Without such a framework, the investigator is reliant on all of the appropriate data being gathered and then somehow being able to synthesise this into a coherent final hypothesis.

The Hypotheses Model can be applied to investigations regardless of context. It may however be appropriate to observe at this point that, for all sorts of reasons, not all bodies charged with investigations want to engage with such a comprehensive model. There are some organisations or bodies that just want to test whether a particular complaint that has been made is supported or not by the evidence and not to delve further into any underlying issues or attendant factors. For investigative bodies like this the hypotheses model may seem complex and unnecessary.

Evidence Gathering Model

In most investigations the notion of a guiding framework is important to; ensure early actions to preserve safety are in place; to direct the evidence gathering process; and to analyse and evaluate the information and evidence. This is particularly the case in those situations that are fast moving, with a scene, when the early stages to eliminate danger and to preserve evidence can be quite chaotic for the investigator. In these cases the hypotheses framework cannot totally eliminate the chaotic nature but it should enable those in charge to focus on their priorities through the initial demanding times.

At the early stages of most investigations there is a great deal for the investigator to think about. After first dealing with any threats that may exist and making the investigation field safe, the investigator has to concentrate on securing vital evidence that can be so easily lost at the early stages. During this time many people are acting in irrational and uncoordinated ways. Experience tends to show that there is no way to totally remove the chaos or to completely reduce the high level of complexity. However, if the person in charge is working to a well defined strategy such as the hypotheses with a clear set of priorities, it is possible to manage that chaos. It could be argued that a lengthy list may not be useful in this regard.

One of the best things that the investigator can do is to apply as simple as possible approach to the identification, securing and gathering of evidence or information. To assist this it is possible to use a relatively simple evidence gathering model. Investigators can consider that the evidence they seek comes from any one of four sources: these can be labelled; **Human** sources, the **Environment**, **Records** and **Objects**. This fact should enable them to identify evidence in specific contexts. Therefore, the evidence gathering model can be represented by a four letter mnemonic:

Human Sources

Environment

Records

Objects.

This section will outline the details of evidence from these different sources, provide some observations about the strength of each of the sources and show how the model can be used to assess the accuracy and veracity of information. It will reemphasise the level of care that is needed to avoid the kind of misinterpretation or inappropriate weighting that can occur through the patterning process that was explained in Section One of the book. This will particularly be the case for human source but equally where human source interpretation of other sources of evidence is critical.

Human Sources

Human Source evidence is perhaps the least reliable of the four sources and yet it has been given a fairly high level of importance in most review settings; be they court hearings, tribunals or even individual consultations. The people who comprise this source of evidence can be divided into two categories; 'Eye Witnesses' and 'Specialists'. Eye witnesses are those people have directly witnessed an incident, part of it or activity preceding or following it. The 'Specialist' category includes those people who can offer professional comment on any aspect of the evidence or information from the hypotheses content.

Eye Witnesses

Section One of this book has identified the limitations of accounts from those who might be categorised as eye witnesses. There is a strong possibility that all or part of their accounts may have been the result of psychological influences such as patterning, that cause it to become corrupted and therefore less reliable. Of course there are those people who may have been involved in the event who are at legal jeopardy and they may have a reason to deliberately mislead an investigator. It should however be clarified that not every witness provides inaccurate accounts and they may be able to provide an account that matches the level of accuracy as the one given by Charles Michael JACKSON in the earlier case study.

However, the key tasks for the investigator in respect to this category of human source evidence are firstly to gather all of the information and evidence that they have; and secondly to try to determine what parts of their information relates to the actual event and what may be a product of the kinds of 'patterning' processes outlined in the earlier section. With eye witnesses, victims and suspects, success in these aims can be maximised by employing skilled interviewers who can use the most appropriate methods and up to date protocols for the given circumstances. Where the interviewee is traumatised, young, mentally impaired etc. and has particular needs the interview strategy will be designed to gain the most information in a way that is acceptable to any one scrutinising the investigation. Clearly it would not be practicable here to provide a comprehensive account of the interview methodologies and protocols and there are many publications that can be referred to.

It may however be worth reiterating that the interview strategy should be designed not only to cater for the interviewees needs but also to gain information that will help to test one or more of the working hypotheses. For instance, to test a hypothesis involving criminal or unlawful conduct the witness should be asked questions that explore deliberate acts and the intentions of the wrongdoer.

As well as testing the content of one or more hypotheses, the investigator should be looking for information that reveals evidence from any of the other categories. For example, the witness can be asked about any objects that may have been touched and could potentially yield fingerprint or DNA evidence. They could be asked about the presence of anything that might present a record of the events or of someone's behaviour or they could be asked about details of the environment or the witnesses position within it; this would help to assess lines of sight or issues of visibility.

When considering who can help with their investigation, it may be fairly straight forward for the investigator to identify those people who are known, present or forthcoming; however they should bear in mind those potential witnesses who are not so obvious and it goes without saying that offenders are not likely to be so forthcoming. Some however may have been in the area and not yet identified.

To identify those less obvious human sources the investigator should look for indications that people were present. These indications can take many forms, for instance; signs that delivery men may have called nearby such as leaflets in the letter boxes; well kept gardens where people have obviously spent time; sets of scaffolding or signs of recent DIY (do-it-yourself) activity; use of telephone boxes or ATM (automated teller machines).

There may be times when the victim is not present or traceable. It should not be assumed when one victim is located that there are no others. Where there are signs of injury the investigator may use DNA analysis to determine whether there is more than one person injured. In other cases and in these circumstances the investigator may look for similar indications used for witnesses. The process of tracing individuals is considered a key element of most investigations but there is more to consider when they have been identified.

61

The first section of the book and preceding paragraphs has highlighted the fragility of witness testimony from a psychological perspective but the investigator must not overlook the physiological considerations. The investigator should consider such things as how good the person's eyesight is, how well they hear, how good they are at judging distance, height, speed etc. These details can provide the investigator with an opportunity to determine whether such things can support or detract from the accuracy of the evidence or accounts that they are receiving.

On most occasions, it is useful to conduct a quick skills and knowledge assessment of the person. If, for example the witness talks about seeing an object such as a weapon, supplementary questions may include their experience in seeing or identifying these sorts of items. If they report seeing something from a particular place it may be worth checking to determine whether they would be afforded such a view for that position. Of course, the opportunities to trace individuals and the kind of skills assessment needed depend largely on the circumstances and the investigator should be alert to features or situations that are relevant to any aspect of their hypotheses.

Specialist

The category 'Specialist' includes any person who is suitably qualified to examine or to comment on any of the working hypotheses or any evidential element of those hypotheses. The important part of this definition is the need for the specialist to be a qualified person and the investigator should ensure that the person, department or organisation undertaking the task is suitably qualified.

Many people are prepared to comment on technical issues from a non-qualified position. A useful example occurs in the training of investigators when they are shown a letter that is found at the scene of a hanging. The letter is written in a foreign language and the students have been warned about the dangers of taking notice of non-qualified observers. Despite these warnings, there are always one or two students who want to translate the letter. When asked about their qualifications to do so, they often cite dated secondary school learning.

The example is not meant to denigrate well-intended people who wish to forward the enquiries but to emphasise the natural tendency for people to make assessments based on limited knowledge. The experience in the classroom is also mirrored in real situations and the investigator should take trouble to determine a persons qualifications.

The first part of the book and the earlier paragraphs of this section have focussed on the 'patterning' process involved in people's interpretation of data. It should be reinforced that 'specialists' are not immune from this psychological phenomenon. The added difficulty for specialists is that many of the patterns of the type referred to are included under the label 'theory'. Not all theories are beyond rebuttal and experience shows that, in formal hearings, there are a large number of occasions where one specialist is enlisted to refute the assessment of another.

It could be argued that it is the specialist's role to provide the investigator with facts and not to make sweeping conclusions such as the one made by the pathologist in the old man case study. In his assessment he states *"The appearances would be consistent with the history of a road traffic accident."* This seems to be beyond his remit and potentially misleading for the investigator. The key question for the investigator is not whether it is consistent with that hypothesis but whether it is inconsistent with the other working hypotheses; how, for example, are the injuries inconsistent with the old man tripping and falling, collapsing and striking the ground or being hit over the head by a third party.

The investigator can gain most from specialist assessment of evidence by sharing their hypotheses and asking the specialist how the

63

evidence is inconsistent with any of them.   It is unlikely that the assessment of a single piece of evidence could totally disprove a hypothesis but on occasions, it may go some way to doing so. A useful example may be the assessment that an individual could not have inflicted the injuries on themselves would go a long way to ruling out the suicide hypothesis. To minimise the introduction of patterns into specialist evidence the investigator can limit the amount of detail of the circumstances that they provide to the specialist.

Environment

Environmental conditions can provide a valuable source of evidence for the investigator. The term 'environment' is wide reaching but circumstances of the case will help the investigator to determine what environmental factors are relevant to their case and again the hypotheses and their contents should form the basis for their assessment. The investigator should consider the content and then determine which of the details relates to or can be tested by elements of the environment. Obvious features of the environment include lighting, temperature, visibility etc.

There are however less obvious elements; take for example the cases commonly termed 'cot death' where an infant has been found dead in a cot or bed.   Premature assessment tends to consider the cause to be connected to the phenomena 'sudden infant death syndrome'. Skilled investigators will undoubtedly consider the potential that the child was affected by an environmental factor such as carbon monoxide from a faulty heating system. While the quantity of gasses may be imperceptible to adults, they could be lethal to a newly born child.

When considering environmental issues, what is present may be self evident to the observant and skilled investigator, however, it is also important to consider what may be missing from the environment. Consider the example of the infant death where 'neglect' may be one of the hypotheses; the absence of appropriate nourishment in the cupboards or of adequate clothing or protection against the cold will be of significance to the investigator.

If the environment cannot be assessed at or near the time of the incident and has to be revisited later, care should be taken to ensure that the time corresponds as much as possible with that of the incident. It would not be appropriate, for instance, on Friday night to revisit the scene of a stabbing at a nightclub that occurred the night before when there might well be a different client base and different atmosphere. Similar reasoning could be applied to events where lighting may be an issue; visiting the scene of a collision on an afternoon to assess visibility may be misleading when the collision occurred in the morning when the sun was at a different position in the sky.

The investigator should be able to secure most internal environments and preserve the relevant evidence. However, they should be conscious that even in a relatively short time between the incident and the securing of the environment things might have changed. In one case, on a cold night, an elderly resident of a nursing home was issued with tranquilisers and the windows of the room were opened causing the lady to die from hyperthermia. When police attended, the first thing they did was to close the windows and any chance of assessing the temperature of the room was lost. Other examples have included replacing phones, turning down sound and seemingly following a natural tendency in someway to want to clean things up.

The investigator should try to establish whether anything has been changed by attendees and look for any signs that such changes may have taken place. Clearly, there will be occasions where things have needed to be changed to preserve safety but in all other cases, there should be an encouragement to leave things as they are until the appropriate specialists can be called.

A useful means of assessing changes to an environment is to seek the views of a person who is familiar with that environment. A good example of this was the case involving Jeremy Bamber (1986) where evidence the normal state of the premises provided the police with useful areas to test. If the investigator uses a person familiar with the specific environment, they should ensure that they have first been eliminated from their enquiries.

A variation on this line of enquiry is to use someone who is familiar with the type of environment for example if the incident is in a factory someone familiar with that type of setting may be more able to spot things that are out of place or do not belong. This assessment will be based on the person's interpretation of the environment, as they know it and appropriate weighting should be given to the information received.

The constantly changing nature of the outside environment will mean that the investigator may encounter difficulties in capturing evidence in a timely fashion. He or she may have to rely on the accounts and descriptions provided by witnesses or first persons at the location. In doing so, they should understand the frailties of recall and interpretation. They should always consider cross referencing other sources of evidence to help them to assess the real nature of the environment. As an example a person might report the air temperature as '*very cold*' but thermometers record temperatures that would normally be classed as 'mild'.

Records

In respect to the investigation model, records include any permanent record that represents human behaviour. Prior to the spread of technology they were mostly in written format such as notes letters and ledgers. In today's world similar records may be in computer format, on a mobile phone or some electronic management system. Take for example a note left by a suicide victim; in the past, this was likely to be a hand written note; now it may take the form of a mobile phone text message, a computer email or even an entry in an internet social networking site such as MySpace or Facebook.

The investigator should think widely about the potential of 'record' evidence in relation to investigations, in previous cases this has included such things as tachograph readings from heavy goods vehicles, engine management systems and vehicle location technology. The photo shows the dials of a crashed vehicle and the speedometer needle that has locked in position on collision. Specialists can identify that this is likely to have been the speed of the vehicle at the time of impact. In the case of the earlier case study, CCTV provided a reliable visual account of the  movements of the old man, sufficient to test the accounts of the witnesses.

There is little doubt that 'record' evidence is far more reliable than that of eyewitnesses, however, care should be taken on how the records are interpreted. The soundless pictures of CCTV may on some occasions be straightforward to understand, this was the case with the old man crossing the road in the earlier case study. However, an apparent argument between two people without the sound could also be a playful interchange between the two; or an apparently friendly arm round the shoulder may disguise a vicious threat. In a similar vein, consistent inaccurate entries in financial bookkeeping may not prove a case of fraud or disprove the hypothesis that there was consistent and clumsy errors by the bookkeeper.

In the Old man case study, the trainee investigators are presented with the dilemma of the conflicting stories about his direction of travel. The CCTV pictures clearly solve that problem for them. However if the CCTV was not available they would see, from the scene, that he had with him a bag of shopping. The bag would contain a number of items, some stamped with the shop price tags. Present also might be till receipts each with a recorded time and date that the shopper visited the store.

The records would provide the investigator with an opportunity to identify his last visited store and from that, they may be able to deduce his direction of travel. If the receipts showed that he had visited a shop on the café side of Station Road one minute before the time of the collision (as identified by the lorry tachograph), using an approximated walking speed they have a better chance of testing which of the accounts of his direction of travel was accurate.

The case study shows examples of how records provide evidence and allow other source information to be tested. However, in this case there are a number of assumptions about these records that need to be clarified before the evidence can be ratified. The first is to ensure that the times on the till receipts, the CCTV and the tachograph in the lorry are in accord with the actual time of day. The best  way to do this would be to calibrate them against Greenwich Mean Time through the British Telecom Speaking Clock. Secondly, it is necessary to ensure that it was in fact the old man who visited the shops and purchased the items.

When validated each of these records provides the investigator with a more reliable means of assessing the human source evidence but the case highlights how even seemingly straightforward data needs to be checked for accuracy and that any interpretation of the data is based on fact not assumption. The investigator should also remain conscious of the need to employ the appropriate people when specialist analysis is required.

The investigator should not only consider the records that are present in the particular enquiry but also the absence of any records that would be expected to be kept in the circumstances. If for example, in an industrial injury case, there are comprehensive records of machinery maintenance for a number of years, which suddenly stop prior to the injury the investigator will need to explore the reasons the records stopped. There may be similar issues in any case where the keeping of records is compulsory or best practice and yet they are absent; cases of fraud and embezzlement are typical.

Objects

This category reveals evidence that is potentially the most reliable of the four sources. This category includes any physical thing that is capable of forensic analysis; in the case of death or physical injury, this would include the body of the victim. The reliability of this evidence stems from two factors. Firstly, the actual presence of an object in a particular place at a particular time can be irrefutable. Clearly, the enquiry will need to focus on how it came to be there and what significance it has to the investigation, but its mere presence if proved is an undeniable fact.

The second issue of reliability comes from the fact that almost all analysis of objects is scientifically based and a significant amount of reliability can be placed on correctly conducted scientific examination. Scientific evidence yields the two pieces of evidence that can be considered conclusive if the related tests are carried out correctly; these are fingerprint evidence and mechanical fit.

To date it has not been disproved that each individual has a unique set fingerprints. Therefore, it can be assessed that an individual's fingerprints being found on an object at a location will mean that that person has come into contact with that item. If the item is fixed in a place then equally it can assessed that that person was in that place at some time.

 The second conclusive piece of evidence stems from the principle of 'mechanical fit'. This principle is based on the fact that when an item fractures into pieces, only pieces from the original item will mechanically fit together. It is accepted that there is no possibility that a piece of material from another item could mechanically fit with the evidence.

In both fingerprint evidence and mechanical fit evidence highlighted above it is useful to apply a principle expounded by the philosopher Karl Popper that tends to advocate that a theory can only be disproved. It is summed up well through the following observation:

"The problem, in basic terms, can be understood by example: given that the sun has risen every day for as long as anyone can remember, what is the rational proof that it will rise tomorrow? How can one rationally prove that past events will continue to repeat in the future, just because they have repeated in the past? While there is no way to prove that the sun will rise, we can formulate a theory that every day the sun will rise, if it does not rise on some particular day, our theory will be disproved but at present it is confirmed. Since it is a well-tested theory, we have every right to believe that it accurately represents reality, so far as we know".

Stephen Hawking adds to this debate by stating:

"No matter how many times the results of an experiment agree with some theory, you can never be sure that the next time the result will not contradict the theory."

In terms of the fingerprint theory and the mechanical fit principle, there has been nothing to date disclosed to disprove them and it is reasonable for the investigator to believe that they hold true and in this sense they can have faith in the evidence, if the analysis is carried out correctly.

Some commentators will conclude that, apart from identical twins, Deoxyribonucleic acid (DNA) can be considered unique in the same way fingerprints are. However, forensic scientists are likely to give a ratio value for 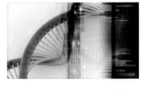 DNA findings such as 1 in 10 million of the population will have this DNA. In a country of 60 million, statistically, there could be another five people with the same DNA; unlikely but statistically possible.

The fingerprint and mechanical fit evidence and to some extent the DNA evidence are well tested and the investigator can have some confidence in them. However, some theories are less rigorous and the investigator should apply the appropriate weighting from any conclusions derived from them. A useful example of this cited earlier was the case of Professor Roy Meadows. He endorsed the dictum that *"one sudden infant death is a tragedy, two is suspicious and three is murder, until proved otherwise"* in his book ABC of Child Abuse and this became known as Meadow's Law and at one time was widely adopted by social workers and child protection agencies (such as the NSPCC) in Britain.

Of course, it is difficult for the investigator to second-guess a specialist and question their theories, but they should be alert to the risk of drawing huge conclusions from one source of evidence and closing down all hypotheses that do not accord with it. Each piece of evidence should be considered as one part of the overall puzzle and whilst some pieces are larger and more significant than others the investigator has to be confident that he or she has enough of the pieces or that enough of the expected pieces are absent to be able to close a hypothesis.

Karl Popper's notion that theories can only be disproved is one useful principle for investigators to apply. Another useful principle is that of Dr Edmond Locard (1877-1966) Locard's exchange principle. Paul Kirk 1953 sums this up succinctly:

Wherever he steps, wherever he touches, whatever he leaves, even without consciousness, will serve as a silent witness against him. Not only his fingerprints or his footprints, but his hair, the fibres from his clothes, the glass he breaks, the tool mark he leaves, the paint he scratches, the blood or semen he deposits or collects. All of these and more bear mute witness against him. This is not absent because human witnesses are. It is factual evidence. Physical evidence cannot be wrong, it cannot perjure itself, it cannot be wholly absent. Only human failure to find it, study it and understand it can diminish its value.

This contact principle should help the investigator to identify which objects may be relevant to the investigation and applicable to any of the working hypotheses. The role of the investigator is to preserve this evidence, have it professionally analysed and determine its impact one of more of their working hypotheses. The caution is in the last sentence of the above quote *"Only human failure to find it, study it and understand it can diminish its value."*

In the categories of 'human source' and 'record' evidence, the investigator is encouraged to consider people or records that are not present but the observable signs that they may have been. The same principle applies to objects that may be missing from the scene of the investigation. The photograph shows the light patch on the grass that  indicates that an object was there recently or the possibly missing knife from the rack. These objects may or may not be relevant to the  investigation but it would be incumbent on the investigator to eliminate them from any of the hypotheses. Other useful examples of this might include dust marks on furniture or indentations on carpeted floors etc. Clearly, these examples are not exhaustive but the important thing is that the investigator is alert to any signs of missing objects that may be relevant.

There are a number of issues that the investigator should take great care of when dealing with 'object' source evidence. These include the following:

• The majority of object evidence is static but fragile. Fingerprints and DNA material can be disturbed if exposed to the elements or handled clumsily. Fragments, items, soils, and footprints are equally vulnerable. The important points for the investigator are to identify as early as possible the relevant objects or trace evidence and secure them from interference.

• The evidence can easily become corrupted particularly where individual investigators move across different areas of the investigation field or come into contact with a number of objects within them. The investigator should be extremely diligent in keeping cross contamination to an absolute minimum.

- The objects should be recovered and packaged in a way that does not hamper the analysis that is required. It would not be possible in this book to provide comprehensive directions for the variety of objects that the investigator might come across. On most occasions the analysis will require specialists and a good rule of thumb is to consult them about the best methods of recovery and packaging.

- Continuity is of paramount importance. The investigator must be able to show an interrupted chain link in relation to the specific object. He must be able to demonstrate that the object recovered from the investigation is the same object that went for analysis; is the same one that was returned from analysis; is the same one that was shown to witnesses; is the same one that was produced at the court/tribunal/ hearing etc. The best way to achieve this uninterrupted chain is by unique numbers for every item and continuity statements if anyone takes possession of the item for any reason.

- Recovery and analysis of an object should, where possible, be controlled and planned. Without doubt there will be times where recovery has to be spontaneous, particularly where is threatened by the circumstances such as weather or personal interference. However, in terms of analysis the rule is that non-destructive examination is carried out before any destructive analysis. Consider the note mentioned earlier at the scene of the hanging; it is important to read and photograph the note (non-destructive method) before it is treated with chemicals to identify the ink or the presence of fingerprints (destructive methods). Whenever possible the investigator is advised to consult with the specialists involved and agree a strategy for recovery and analysis of identified objects.

Application of the HERO Model

The HERO model is intended primarily to help simplify the identification of evidence in complex situations. It provides the investigator with a framework that should broaden their consideration about where to find the evidence that will help them to test their working hypotheses. In the first instance, each of the sources will yield primary evidence.

The model can also be used to cross-reference information and evidence from the different sources to test their veracity, identify similarities and pinpoint discrepancies (see Fig 8 below). Using the model in this way allows the investigator to identify the primary sources and to employ the cross reference method as a support process. It is particularly useful in testing the less reliable evidence and information from Human Sources with the more reliable evidence of Records and Objects.

It should be emphasised that where there is similarity in information from different sources, it does not mean that it is factually correct. In the Old Man Case Study a number of eye witnesses gave similar accounts that were inaccurate. However where there are discrepancies the investigator is almost duty bound to enquire about them and understand what has caused them to be different.

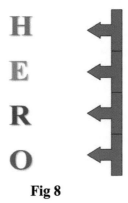

Fig 8

As can be seen from the case study a number of eyewitnesses provide very similar accounts but these are contradicted by one witness. Using the recorded evidence from CCTV and possibly the evidence from the shopping bag to cross-reference the accounts the more accurate account in relation to the movements of the old man can be identified with more certainty. Similarities from one type of source may not provide an accurate picture for example a number of records may be forged to reflect the same position but cross-referenced with accounts from people (human source evidence) or the forensic analysis of the documents themselves (object evidence) may identify discrepancies and flaws in the forged records.

It cannot be emphasised enough that the job of the investigator is to determine the 'facts'. However, as can be seen from the case study and experiences of the author, establishing what is fact, what is interpretation form a persons patterns or what is limited theory from a specialist can be a complex process. It is this writer's standpoint that the investigator should assume nothing; test everything; and document findings and processes as comprehensively as possible. The HERO Model provides the investigator with a simple model that will enable them to gather as much evidence as is possible in their endeavour to establish facts.

In terms of priorities of evidence it can be seen that the most reliable is the presence of physical objects and the forensic evidence that can be gained from them. Next reliable are records such as CCTV, computers or written documents. Then in terms of reliability the Environment and lastly Human Sources. However, the investigator must also take into account time and opportunity issues in capturing the evidence. If witnesses are leaving the scene quickly, some means of recording their identities must be considered; by the same token if the environment is unstable but crucial to one or more of the hypotheses or it has the potential to destroy forensic evidence, steps to record it and provide protection are necessities. The priorities will be dependent on the attendant circumstances and dictated by the strategy.

Summary

The book is aimed at the professional bodies whose members are tasked with complex levels of investigation. However, anyone who wishes to carry out comprehensive investigation will find the outlined methods and model extremely useful in directing their enquiries and providing them a framework from which to work.

It is identified that the way individuals process and interpret information, events and situations is one of the issues that have frustrated many investigations in the past and will undoubtedly continue to do so in the future.

Human beings process every piece of data and endeavour to link it with a previous experience that they have had or that they have learned about from others. Much of this linking process occurs out of the consciousness of the person and as Edward De Bono terms it, the brain is a self-organising system. Each experience or piece of learning causes the individual to create a pattern in their minds; when they see, hear or even feel things that are similar to the experience they tend to make the connection.

The simple example of the chair is used within the text. Our teacher sits in chairs many times a day throughout her life and she learns to accept, without thinking about it, that the chair is something that she can sit on and will bear her weight; she has formulated the 'pattern' of a chair. That pattern holds true until she walks into the classroom of Form 3A, where some students have mocked up a broken chair that collapses when she goes to sit on. From this point, she formulates a new pattern of chair. This new pattern is applied in the context of Form 3A; undoubtedly, given similar circumstances she will test the chair before she sits on it.

In the investigative world a similar sort of process will occur. For example, the Coroners Officer tasked with investigating deaths will view the death of an elderly person in their home with no obvious violence certified by a medical practitioner, as 'natural causes'. This is as much a 'pattern' as the one of a chair. The pattern will endure until the Coroner's Officer sees that the elderly person lives alone, each time the same Doctor is present at the time of death or immediately before and on each occasion the elderly person has bequeathed the doctor some of their estate. With supporting evidence, the Coroner will create a new pattern in relation to elderly deaths and question whether the next one might be 'another victim of serial killer'. This new pattern will, in future cases, stimulate the officer to enquire about the Doctors timely presence, ask about medication issued by him and perhaps request toxicology tests at the post mortem. Many of these enquiries may not have been deemed necessary prior to his or her new experience and formulated pattern.

The investigator will encounter this patterning process in most people that they seek evidence from in the course of their enquiries. Eyewitnesses are likely to provide a varying mix of details that they have seen during the incident and details from their 'patterns'. The range of variation from person to person is evident in the Old Man Case Study; from Charles JACKSON who provides a highly accurate account of the event to Francis MORRIS who provides details that could not be further from the mark.

Specialists are the next category of persons who contribute to an investigation. These are people, who are qualified to comment on technical aspects of the investigation and might be expected to be free from the patterning process. Regrettably, this is not always the case and at times, the patterns are even more ingrained and protected under the heading 'theory'. The text has cited examples of specialist theories that have proved to be far less reliable than first assessed. In the case study there is clear evidence of patterning when the pathologist comment that the injuries are consistent with the history (*and here read pattern*) of a road traffic accident.

The key person in the investigation whose interpretation against a particular pattern can be highly detrimental to an effective investigation is the investigator. It is not difficult to understand how repetitive experiences or strong socialisation can cause the investigator to conclude that the hanging is a 'suicide'; the cot death is 'sudden infant death syndrome'; the injuries on the building site are 'industrial injury'; the lad who absconds form a care home is a 'regular absconder' and not in any danger etc.

The added difficulty with the patterning process is its complexity. Patterns are layered on top of patterns that are layered on top of more patterns. Take the example of Jason JONES, in the case study: he sees the old man lying near the kerb on the Clarks Store side of Station Road and believes that he stepped off that kerb into the path of the lorry just as he has seen on the television safety messages. His mother's account and an even more detailed account by his friend Francis MORRIS reinforce his belief. Add to this the possibility that he has been taught by his parents not to contradict adults in the presence of others. Include his possible belief that going against his pal may jeopardise their relationship; listening to his mother provide her account to the police and the feeling that she is experienced and probably right. Take the police officer who gives him choices "*did you stop before the crossing or after it?*" and the possibility that he has been taught to co-operate and help the police; add to that his experience at school where multiple choice questions always have a right answer.

There is no way of knowing if any of the speculation with regards to the patterns applied by this witness is accurate but it is not difficult to see how the multi layered patterns can unconsciously conspire to corrupt evidence. The difficult role of the investigator is to determine what is 'fact' and what is the 'product of patterns'.

The further difficulty with patterns is that on many occasions' things turn out to be exactly in line with the individual's patterns and what they assessed them to be in the first place. In these cases people can wonder what all the fuss is about and why there was any doubt. However, every so often, the individual will find out that they have things completely wrong. Whilst, day to day, this presents a learning opportunity but little problem for the individual, in the world of investigation it can have serious implications. Perhaps most worrying are the times where the individual does not know whether they have got it right or wrong and carrying on in blissful ignorance assuming that their pattern was correct and reinforcing it for the future.

Given the complexity and difficulties with the patterning process by the investigator, it would be understandable if he or she were encouraged to work from a blank canvas, harvest all possible evidence, and then make a final conclusion. At the time of printing this book at least one investigative doctrine issued to British Police Forces, advocated just that approach. Investigators were advised not to formulate hypotheses until they had gathered all of the evidence.

There are however, a number of valid reasons why that approach could not and should not be adopted; these are summarised as follows:

- There is absolutely no possibility that individuals could stop the patterning process. It is the way that they interpret data every day of their lives and every waking minute of those days. It would be virtually impossible to function if their mind questioned every piece of stimulus before they reacted. As has been stated much of this mental activity takes place out of consciousness, it is an automatic process and it would be a huge feat to somehow change it.

- Without patterns (hypotheses) there would be nothing to stimulate the investigator to look for evidence that was not immediately obvious to him. For example, without the hypotheses that a missing child may have been harmed by its parents or had some form of accident in its home, there would be nothing to stimulate preservation of the house and a forensic search. It could be argued that this might come to light freely later in the investigation, but by then any attempts to gather evidence would be too late.

- The experiences of the investigators enable them to formulate a comprehensive set of hypotheses and to understand the wide range of details that each hypothesis might contain. As they have new experiences or consult with different people, they will widen this understanding. Each piece of content provides the investigator with a line of enquiry that will help them to test the viability of the hypothesis.

Section Two of the book proposes the Hypotheses Model as a methodology that discourages the formulation of premature conclusions but utilises the knowledge and experience of the investigator and the members of his or her team.

Firstly, the model advocates that, from the receipt of the first substantial information, the investigator lists each of the hypotheses that could be applicable in the presenting circumstances. Secondly, it encourages him/her to use their experience and knowledge to consider all of the content that might make up the identified working hypothesis. To broaden those details the investigator should involve members of their team and any specialists who are qualified to comment on all or part of the hypothesis or its content. Having prepared the investigation strategy in this way, they can set actions to determine whether the evidence supports the content or whether significant elements are missing thereby reducing the viability of any one of the hypotheses.

The first principle of the Hypotheses Model is that the investigator seeks to disprove the hypotheses and not to try to prove them. He or she may arrive at a position where they can disprove all of the hypotheses except one but still not be able to prove that hypothesis. This quite often happens in the case of suicide where murder, manslaughter and accident can be disproved but suicide cannot be proved. In such circumstances, it would be safe for the investigator to conclude that this can be the only possibility.

The second principle is that the investigator lists the Hypotheses at the outset of the investigation and works to disprove each of them simultaneously (in parallel) and not one after the other (in series). Applying the 'in series' method has the risk that the priority lines of enquiry for some of the hypotheses are delayed. The parallel working ensures that interventions are timely and makes best use of, what can be at times, limited resources.

The Hypotheses Model can be used at any stage of the investigation. Primarily it will be used to formulate the initial hypotheses but it could be used to equal value on a specific hypothesis or on an ancillary enquiry such as the earlier case of the motorcyclist, where the cause of his death was the main investigation and the presence of heroin in his blood and ancillary issue. The process of applying the model at this later stage should not necessitate gathering evidence all over again, merely a reassessment of the existing information or evidence.

There may be times where all of the chosen hypotheses can all be disproved or where information or evidence is forthcoming that does not apply to the working hypotheses. In these cases it will be incumbent on the investigator to accept that there was a hypothesis that was not considered and that should now be added to the enquiry.

The section outlines the **HERO** Evidence Gathering Model. This will help the investigator to be able to gather relevant evidence even in the most complex situations. Experience shows that evidence comes from four main sources; **H**uman sources, the **E**nvironment, **R**ecords and **O**bjects. These sources will yield primary evidence but they can also be used to cross-reference information and evidence from any of the other sources to test their veracity. This cross-referencing process is particularly valuable when assessing whether evidence from a human source is actual fact or whether it is a product of the patterning process.

By adopting the Hypotheses Model and HERO the investigators have a greater chance of conducting the efficient, effective and transparent investigation that is often sought. Clear articulation of their methodology allows comprehensive review of their work and encourages critical interventions from other parties.

The book does not pretend to provide the investigator with a catchall list of actions that will result in a thorough investigation. The investigator cannot be, nor should they try to be, a specialist in every field of the investigation, it is far better to use the qualified people who will all have their own manuals and protocols to provide them with the most up to date methods and techniques.

This does not mean that the investigator should abrogate all responsibility to the 'specialist'. The cross-referencing process in HERO may well reveal evidence that appears to contradict a specialist and the investigator should feel confident enough to test these discrepancies against a well-formulated strategy.

Some bodies that are charged with investigation do not wish to conduct such a comprehensive investigation. They see their role as determining whether the matter that is complained about is supported or not. They may not be concerned with the reasons for the allegation/complaint, whether some other related issue or whether there is a systemic problem. For these people the Hypotheses Model may seem overly complicated for their needs. They may be content to work through each point of the alleged issue to determine whether it is supported or not by the evidence and delivering a judgement on that basis. These bodies should find the HERO Model useful in that respect.

One of the most important things that the Hypotheses Model does is to enable the investigators to satisfy themselves and any critical observer that any other plausible explanation has been explored and that questions about them can be answered. There will be times when an investigator cannot arrive at a definitive conclusion; where he or she cannot eliminate all but one of the hypotheses but the open and transparent process will allow for a comprehensive review.

There will be investigators who consider that their experience and expertise will allow them to draw early conclusions and may feel that the methodology and model is potentially time consuming and costly. In response to that, it may be worth providing the full quote from one investiagtor, an extract of which appears at the beginning of the book. He said:

"Of course experienced and competent investigators will often use their professional judgement. However, they will always consider that it is better to **assess** *that something is the case than to* **assume** *it to be so.... it is my experience that a shortcut more often turns out to be the longest, most complex and painful route to take.*

If you consider that time and resources are an issue, you can rest assured that, when needed the powers that be will find sufficient of both to review your work.

The issues that you investigate matter to people and substandard work on your part may hinder their ability to move on in their lives and can erode the faith that they have in a system that they feel is designed to protect them. This can have far reaching consequences for all of us"

9947121R00048

Printed in Great Britain
by Amazon.co.uk, Ltd.,
Marston Gate.